THE JAPANESE TALMUD

CHRISTOPHER L. SCHILLING

The Japanese Talmud

Antisemitism in East Asia

HURST & COMPANY, LONDON

First published in the United Kingdom in 2023 by
C. Hurst & Co. (Publishers) Ltd.,
New Wing, Somerset House, Strand, London, WC2R 1LA
Copyright © Christopher L. Schilling, 2023
All rights reserved.

A Cataloguing-in-Publication data record for this book
is available from the British Library.

ISBN: 9781787389540

www.hurstpublishers.com

To Daniel

CONTENTS

ACKNOWLEDGEMENTS

The Japanese Talmud became possible with the generous financial support of the Japanese Society for the Promotion of Science (JSPS), the Korean National Research Foundation (NRF), and the Fritz Thyssen Foundation. Parts of Chapter 1 have previously appeared in: 'Jewish Seoul: An Analysis of Philo- and Antisemitism in South Korea', *Modern Judaism—A Journal of Jewish Ideas and Experience*, 38(2), May 2018, pp. 183–97; and parts of Chapter 2 in: 'On Symbolic Philosemitism in Japan', *Journal of Modern Jewish Studies*, 19(3), pp. 297–313. I am grateful to have had the opportunity to conduct research for this book as a visiting scholar at Seoul National University, National Chengchi University, and the University of Tsukuba. I'm particularly thankful to Myoung-Kyu Park and Kenichi Ishii for hosting me. I am grateful to Frank Joseph Shulman, an editor and consultant for reference publications in Asian Studies and a former associate editor of the *Bibliography of Asian Studies*, published by the Association for Asian Studies, Inc., for providing me with useful background information for the book. I'm impressed by his integrity, kindness, and dedication to scholarship. Finally, I am thankful to the anonymous reviewers of the manuscript, as well as Daniel Allenstein, who took the time to read and comment on this book. He is as a reader as he is as a friend: kind, supportive, and insightful. Naturally, any omissions are mine. Immense thanks are also due to the folks at Hurst, especially Michael Dwyer, Lara Weisweiller-Wu and Mei Jayne Yew, for their fantastic editing, as well as to Anna Benn for her thoughtful copy-editing.

INTRODUCTION

Within a couple of miles south of Taipei's city centre with its
skyscrapers and the Taipei 101, once the world's tallest building,
National Chengchi University is tucked away between cloudy
mountains as picturesque as a Chinese brush painting. But instead
of graceful pagodas and bamboo huts, what appears are concrete
blocks, bubble tea cafés, and hardware shops. To complete the
scenic picture, one would have to climb the area's mountains to
find behind their clouds a scenery of Buddhist and Daoist temples
and Confucian shrines. The colleague I met on my first research
trip to Asia was friendly enough to invite me for lunch on my
first day on campus, but he seemed a little puzzled as to why I
was conducting research on the Jewish people and antisemitism
in East Asia. The reason for his puzzlement became clear as we
sat down at an Italian-style restaurant near the main campus gate.
The well-prepared documents which he had brought to lunch, and
which consisted of a list of the faculty members' current research
projects, made it evident that scientists at his university tended
to study prevailing topics. I, in contrast, was concerning myself
with hate which a mere 0.003 per cent of his country's population
might potentially face.

While we waited for an Asian take on Italian pasta, he seemed
uncertain what to make of my research topic; whether this was
because it seemed difficult to pursue or unimportant to him, I
was unsure. There were certainly language and cultural issues to

1

keep in mind, I knew, and of course the question of who would be interested in reading about my research later on. The food appeared so thoughtfully arranged on the plate that one would have had a hard time describing it as Italian, and my host repeated his earlier question in a single word: 'Jews?' As I had yet to discover the brevity and indirectness of questioning in which East Asians often politely confront a problem, I was unsure how to respond. What I was not prepared for was the formality of debating and a seeming unwillingness to come to any conclusion. There was no direct critique of my ideas as such, instead ever a repetition of the same word no matter how much I explained myself: 'Jews?'

What I was wondering about was the strange paradox of there being a vast admiration of Jews and simultaneously high rates of antisemitism at the eastern end of Asia, a region with almost no Jewish history or presence. The scale on how scholars measure antisemitism in East Asian countries is relatively high.[1] In its 2014 poll, the Anti-Defamation League found South Korea to be among the most antisemitic countries in the non-Muslim world, with 53 per cent of the population harbouring anti-Jewish attitudes (which is only 3 per cent lower than Iran!) It also saw high rates of antisemitism in Japan, at 23 per cent (about as high as in Estonia or Argentina), and the People's Republic of China, at 20 per cent (equivalent to Italy).[2] In Taiwan, the picture is even worse.[3] At the same time, there is a high level of admiration of Jews in East Asia that has led some scholars[4] to describe the region's appreciation of Jewish people in highly philosemitic terms.

At a time that the so-called 'Jewish century'[5] is turning into an 'Asian century',[6] I am immensely fascinated by how Jewish people are seen in East Asia. When I speak of 'East Asia', I refer to China and the countries that were heavily influenced by its culture, most notably Korea and Japan; by 'Westerners', I mean people of European cultural background; and by 'Jews' I mean people who self-identify as being part of the Jewish civilization. A generalization is possible, and meaningful, in this context of the study of thought processes behind antisemitism and the fetishization of Jews, similar to the study of language groups where one can produce scientific knowledge by generally distinguishing between Indo-European languages and East Asian languages. Of course, putting everything into East/West labels without addressing differences in categories such as educational background, age, or gender brings with it the problem of missing the whole picture. Yet, my argument is a generalization because it is precisely meant to give one a general idea of the foundation of antisemitism and a fetishization of Jews in East Asia that is profoundly different to such general phenomena in the West.[7]

How Jews became fetish objects in East Asian countries can be seen with books called 'Talmud', which are bestsellers sold in almost every bookshop (and even some book vending machines) and are even being made part of the public-school curriculum in South Korea. Initially a product of Japan, this so-called 'Talmud' has led to 'Jewish education' institutions opening up in underground shopping malls in Seoul where parents send their children to supposedly improve their IQ. There is an enormous pressure on education in the rapidly changing region of East Asia. As Jews are often portrayed and admired as geniuses in science and business, anything labelled 'Jewish' is viewed as a means of self-development, even though its content may be on Confucianism, the Virgin Mary, the Brothers Grimm, or Goethe. I am interested in what it means to many East Asians when they think of 'Jews', and if it is anything Jewish people themselves would recognize.

But how can societies so obsessed with consuming anything labelled 'Jewish' be at the same time so highly antisemitic? Modern East Asia is not only characterized by a strong focus on education but, unfortunately, also by high levels of loneliness, social isolation, and suicide. I argue that because many members of East Asian societies are becoming increasingly lonely, stereotypical perceptions of antisemitism and philosemitism are being fostered without Jews having any significant presence in the region itself. Interesting in this context is the concept of the stranger in Japanese culture and the development of a legend of the Japanese people being a 'Lost Tribe of Israel'. Of course, belief in this legend is by no means shared by all Japanese. But it is interesting that these kinds of fantasies about Jewish people receive more attention in Japan than factual Jewish-Japanese history such as, for example, the European Jews who fled to Nagasaki in the sixteenth century; or Chiune Sugihara, the 'Japanese Oskar Schindler'; Wolf Isaac Ladejinsky, the 'father' of Japan's highly successful land reform in the late 1940s and early 1950s; and Beate Sirota Gordon, who wrote Articles 14 and 24 of the post-Second World War Japanese Constitution, granting women equal rights to men.

Jewish history in East Asia goes back to the first contact of Jewish people who came to China via the Silk Road and by sea via India during the Tang dynasty (618–907 CE) and subsequently resided in Kaifeng. Their community has not, however, left any significant impact on the region. A more lasting 'idea' of the Jewish people came to East Asia first via Japan with Shakespeare's *The Merchant of Venice*, one of the first foreign plays translated and produced in Japan, as well as *The Protocols of the Elders of Zion*, which became quite popular in Japan at the beginning of the twentieth century although it was evidently an antisemitic forgery. Contemporary Japan, similar to other East Asian countries like China and South Korea, fuses certain antisemitic notions with philosemitic attraction. This dualistic attitude towards Jews has been largely overlooked by other scholars who have focused on Jewish history, or occasionally on cases of antisemitism, in the region.

What makes the Taiwanese case weirdly disturbing is not its 'Talmud Business Hotel' or how well books on 'Jewish' education and business sell in the country, but the lack of respect often displayed towards Jewish historical suffering, exemplified by a Holocaust-themed restaurant that is designed to give customers the experience of eating in a concentration camp (photographs of Auschwitz victims are on the walls, while the toilets are called 'gas chambers'). Moreover, there have been a high number of antisemitic incidents by politicians, companies, and the public, while supporters of Taiwan's current ruling party threatened the Israeli representation should they speak up against antisemitism on the island.[8]

While there is not a single Jewish Studies programme at any of Hong Kong's top institutions of higher education, there was the widespread misuse of the term 'Nazi' during protests in the city. It may come as a surprise that it is a common practice to accuse the other side of being 'Nazis' instead of comparing them to the more obvious historical counterpart of the Japanese occupiers during the Second World War.

Although there is a lack of Holocaust studies programmes across China, some universities on the mainland do host Centres for Jewish Studies. However, apart from occasional antisemitic incidents by some of their scholars, the general impression one gets from these Centres is that they are making the mistake of seeking to understand Judaism only through its religious law and practice, instead of its history of humour, irony, and self-criticism, its philosophy and art. And while China's scholars overvalue Jewish scripture, the general population is, as elsewhere in East Asia, fascinated by Chinese-language versions of Japanese 'Talmud' fabrications.

Using the tools which the study of antisemitism offers to discover the reality behind such fetishization and antisemitism is certainly useful. But to understand this paradoxical phenomenon entirely one must consider the different way East Asian cultures tend to perceive the world. Considering antisemitism in the East Asian context brings difficulties, as the term's existing definitions do not seem to apply properly to the region. Researchers on the phenomenon of unreasonable thoughts towards Jews come from various fields of study such as history, psychology, sociology, theology, and literary studies. What combines these very different ways of approaching the problem is—apart from their being almost entirely produced by Western scholars—a belief in a universal human form of cognitive functioning. Recent research on the mind, however, demonstrates that there is a fundamental difference between Western and Eastern ways of perceiving the world.

People who grew up in an East Asian culture seem to be better at accepting opposing concepts simultaneously. Surprisingly, the study of East Asia demonstrates that it is possible for antisemitism and admiration, or philosemitic love, towards the Jewish people to both exist in a single human mind. Something that appears at first as a cultural misunderstanding, or as being 'lost in translation', can be understood as an expression of the mind that developed in an East Asian cultural context. One cannot understand East Asia without concepts of paradox logic, and one cannot claim to fully understand antisemitism by ignoring how a quarter of the world's population processes cognitive information. By no means am I arguing that East Asians are more antisemitic or less so than people in the West. I propose an argument not in degree but in kind, as this book will demonstrate.

I seek to close a gap in the literature on antisemitism which has, so far, ignored a sizeable amount of the global population, one that supposedly will shape our century to a great extent in the decades to come should the 'Asian century' become a reality. One might argue, due to the lack of a meaningful Jewish presence in East Asia, that antisemitism in this region of the world is a problem with little significance. I disagree, given that we are living in an increasingly interdependent—and also Asian—world, and more importantly because the study of antisemitism is not only of benefit to its direct victims. Rather, it helps us to understand how people—and societies—function and view the world, should they follow this ill-guided way of thinking.

I argue that antisemitism is best described as evil storytelling— as opposed to the common description of it as disease, mental illness, or thoughtless passion—and I wonder how this non-Asian narrative develops in a region shaped by a quite different culture on how to tell a story. Generally speaking, East Asians (compared to Westerners) regard the world as highly changeable, complex, and consisting of interrelated components, and often see events as moving back and forth between extremes. Westerners are inclined to attribute behaviour to the actor, while Asians are prone to attribute behaviour to the context. While Westerners understand the world as being largely static, Easterners see it as more adaptable and constantly changing. East Asians certainly use categories as well, but they are 'less likely to abstract them away from particular objects'.[9] There is the whiteness of snow or the whiteness of silk in ancient Chinese thought, but not whiteness as an abstract which can be applied to things. In Western thought, in contrast, objects have qualities and essences like whiteness, which allow one to confidently predict an outcome or behaviour of the object, independent of its context. Eastern traditional thought, however, takes objects as having concrete properties that interact with their environmental circumstances. There are Jews perceived as somehow evil, and Jews perceived as role models, not 'the Jew' common to Western antisemitic or philosemitic thought processes. In an East Asian way of holistic thinking, nothing exists in an isolated and independent way but rather must be understood in its relationship to context, like musical notes creating a melody in relation to other notes. And so, the concept of Jews perceived in relation to education is different from the concept of Jews perceived in relation to business or politics. Based on these case studies and theorizing, my focus is on the question of how and why East Asians tend to fetishize Jews, which I term *bisemitic*.

After my lunch at the campus restaurant in southern Taipei, my host walked me outside to bow down. He grabbed his umbrella, then said goodbye to me. He looked across campus at the mountains covered in clouds and studied them carefully as if he were looking for an anchor for his thought: 'Jews?'

1

JEWISH SEOUL[1]

The November air is tense with anxiety as a single college entry exam determines the life of Mrs Park's son at his school in South Korea's capital, Seoul. Late students are being escorted to the exam through empty streets with the help of police officers. Traffic stops on the ground and in the air. Sleep-deprived faces are all around her as she waits with other parents at the school gate for the entire nine hours of the exam—praying, hoping, fearing—until her son suddenly comes out. 'I failed,' he says. She wakes up screaming.

When Mrs Park's son was little, she read him books or took him to museums. But when he reached 5 years of age she started to worry about his formal education, fearing that he might suffer in the future because of his perceived lack of education. In South Korea, with its rather extreme focus on education, 83 per cent of 5-year-olds receive private tutoring, and Mrs Park's child is now among the many South Koreans whose effort on education will keep increasing until, at age eighteen, he will take the Suneung exam that determines whether he will be able to enter a top-ranked university or fall behind. Mrs Park shared a deep-rooted worry with probably all Korean parents: what if he does not pass, what if 18 years of education were not enough for him to enter an elite university? Then, she heard of a Jewish 'secret' way to study called the Talmud, and she immediately felt relieved and excited. Had she just discovered a secret path for her son to become a genius?

I'm interested in the strong beliefs held by many South Koreans regarding a group of people they have practically never encountered. There has never been any significant Jewish presence in Korean history until very recently, when the first Jewish community in Korea was established during the Korean War (1950–3). At that time, a couple of hundred Jews from the United States joined the armed forces against North Korea. The 2012 American Jewish Yearbook estimated that there were only about 100 Jews living in South Korea[2] among a South Korean population of about 50 million people. That translates into only about 0.0001 per cent of the South Korean population.

While there are not any known Jews in North Korea, most of the Jews in South Korea, nowadays, reside in Seoul. Most of them work for the US military, or are journalists, exchange students, English teachers, or businesspeople from around the world. Moreover, the Jewish population in South Korea is in constant flux due to the rotation of US military personnel and the fact that most people teaching English in Korea do not stay more than a couple of years. While the Jewish members of the US military in South Korea have a chaplain at the Yongsan Army Base, which restricts most civilians from participating in their religious and cultural activities, the rest of the population relies on one single Chabad Rabbi in Seoul, currently Rabbi Osher Litzman. Chabad is a Hasidic Orthodox outreach movement that sends emissaries to countries around the world. Chabad also operates a kosher store and restaurant in Seoul and ships kosher food via an online shop all over the country. And 'there are many Koreans coming here [Chabad] on a daily basis. They want to learn about Judaism, to buy kosher food, ask questions, [receive] guidance', Rabbi Litzman told the *Jewish Telegraphic Agency* in an interview.[3] There is, however, not a single synagogue in the country, but in 2019, the first *mikveh* (a bath used in Judaism for the purpose of ritual immersion to achieve purity) in South Korea was opened.

With the lack of any academic studies on the topic, South Korea has commonly been described in the media as a philosemitic country, where there are book vending machines selling Korean versions of the Talmud, regular newspapers columns on 'Jewish education', television documentaries on Judaism, and 'Talmudic debates' in schools. On the other hand, an Anti-Defamation League survey found South Korea to be among the most antisemitic countries in the world. This chapter seeks to explain this paradox by taking into account South Korea's rapid transformation over the last decades from one of the poorest to one of the richest countries in the world, the role of education in this process, and the problem of racism in South Korea.

KOREAN SOCIETY AND GLOBALIZATION

At first glance, South Korea has much in common with the State of Israel. Both were founded from scratch in 1948 and have now become high-tech countries and 'start-up nations' despite having no natural resources except for the human capital of highly educated people. Both countries have strong relations with the United States and are democracies bordering a hostile, undemocratic environment. But one should not assume that just because South Korea and the Jewish State have a lot in common, Koreans and Jews also have a lot in common. Indeed, aside from the importance of education in both cultures, they could hardly be more different. The Jewish 'two people, three opinions' is certainly not something that is aspired to, or appreciated, in Korean society.

Even though South Korea has accomplished rapid economic growth over the past decades, with its gross domestic product (GDP) poised to surpass Japan's in the near future, social pressure to succeed has led to many South Koreans suffering from depression. South Korea is, according to recent statistics, the third unhappiest OECD nation in the world, and the unhappiest within Asia.[4] In fact, South Korea has the highest suicide rate of any OECD country, with forty-two South Koreans taking their lives every single day. A 2014 poll found that over half of South Korean teenagers have suicidal thoughts,[5] and, sadly, suicide is currently the leading cause of death among South Korean youth.[6]

11

Many people in South Korea seem to be lost in a rapidly changing world, and are in great need of help to stop their suffering. To give an extreme example, as a way of facing the pressure of modern Korean society, a practice of 'near-death experience' has even started to gain traction in South Korea, where participants stage a 'fake funeral' and engage in what one might call meditation. They put on burial clothes and then lie down in a casket for a while, by which they seek to experience death and reflect on their lives. Thus, in many ways, South Korea appears to be the complete opposite of what Jewish culture could ever, or would ever, produce.

The pressure that so many Koreans feel certainly comes from the expectation to succeed in a fast-paced knowledge economy. South Korea's lack of natural resources is often cited as a reason for its emphasis on education, and the pressure placed on South Korean students is among the greatest in the world. Se-Woong Koo, for instance, wrote in the article, 'An Assault Upon Our Children' that 'the system's dark side casts a long shadow. Dominated by tiger moms, cram schools and highly authoritarian teachers, South Korean education produces ranks of over-achieving students who pay a stiff price in health and happiness. The entire programme amounts to child abuse. It should be reformed and restructured without delay'.[7] Another study found that 81 per cent of middle and high schools forbid romantic relationships among students.[8] In a similar vein, Diane Ravitch warned against a culture of education where children 'exist either to glorify the family or to build the national economy'.[9] It is in relation to this that one finds the very strong interest that Koreans have in Jewish education, and in the Talmud as its perceived source.

THE TALMUD IN SOUTH KOREA

Writing about the Talmud in South Korea makes one reconsider the flexibility of the term 'Talmud'. I have chosen in this chapter to use the term 'Talmud' to refer to Korean books because 'Talmud' is the title they bear, although they are not translations of the Palestinian or the Babylonian Talmud, but collections of rabbinic stories at best. They are usually listed in the 'Religion' section of libraries and bookshops in South Korea. I have also located nine different editions of the Talmud in a bookshop in Manhattan's Koreatown, and Sarit Kattan Gribetz and Claire Kim speak of ten different editions they found in Aladdin Books in Los Angeles' Koreatown, as well as an edition at the Seoul Animation Center's cartoon museum library.[10] Ross Arbes reports in his article in *The New Yorker*[11] of a school for Jewish education just outside of Seoul in which students daily recite the *Shema Israel* in Korean, and have 'Talmudic debates' in class. The students have no intention of converting, nor are their teachers Jewish, nor have most of them ever met a Jew in their lives. But they all share a desire to learn about Jewish education. The founder of the school, Hyunjun Park, was trained at the Shema Education Institute, a Christian institute in Los Angeles that gives Koreans the opportunity to learn how Jews study, pray, and live.

In 2011, Young-sam Ma, the South Korean ambassador to Israel at the time, was interviewed on Israeli television saying:

> I want to show you this! Each Korean family has at least one copy of the Talmud. Korean mothers want to know how so many Jewish people became geniuses. Twenty-three per cent of Nobel Prize winners are Jewish people. Korean women want to know the secret. They found the secret in this book.[12]

The Israeli online newspaper *Arutz Sheva* describes South Korea as having 'more people who read the Talmud—or at least have a copy of it at home—than in Israel'.[13] But whether these Korean 40-pages-or-so versions of the Talmud are quite the same as the original Judaic collection of writings (63 tractates and in standard print over 6,200 pages long) is highly questionable. It also does not make very much sense to study the Talmud without any prior knowledge of the Torah, and even then the Talmud can be a rather challenging read. One could argue that not all of the Talmud is meant to be understood literally, and sections of it deal with outdated practices such as sacrifices, magic, and dream interpretation. Studying the Talmud in Tannaitic Hebrew and Jewish Babylonian Aramaic, one might be struck by the specificity of debated scenarios regarding sacrifices and ritual slaughter,

Jewish civil and criminal law commentary, or legal recitations. It therefore strikes one as surprising that so many South Koreans derive any practical value from this collection of texts.

The Talmud was first made popular in South Korea by Marvin Tokayer, a rabbi who has written many books in East Asia that he calls 'The Talmud'. Someone looking for a copy of the Talmud in South Korea will eventually come across Rabbi Tokayer, as many of the books name him as the author, as well as include a picture of him inside their front covers. His first book, published in Japan and entitled *Five Thousand Years of Jewish Wisdom: Secrets of the Talmud Scriptures*, has gone through about seventy printings and sold about half a million copies in Japan alone. Tokayer went on to publish more than twenty books on Judaism, mainly for the Japanese market, covering topics such as Jewish education, humour, sex dreams, and, of course, the Talmud. For most of these books, Hideaki Kasei served as Tokayer's translator, since he was unable to speak Japanese (or Korean) himself. Hideaki Kasei later became the chairman of the Society for the Dissemination of Historical Facts, which denies Japanese war crimes during the Second World War. David G. Goodman, a professor of Japanese literature, and Masanori Miyazawa, a history professor from Japan, highlighted Tokayer's dependency on Kasei in their book, *Jews in the Japanese Mind: The History and Uses of a Cultural Stereotype*: 'Tokayer cannot read his own work and does not always know what is in it.' With Kasei 'speaking through' Tokayer, they argue that Tokayer's publications lend 'credence to the strangest myths and most stubborn stereotypes of Jews in Japan'.[14]

One only needs to browse through some of Tokayer's published works, such as *There Is No Education in Japan: The Jewish Secret of Educating Geniuses*, to see how he commercialzed Judaism while seemingly ignoring the fact that it could inflame Jewish myths in probably the last regions of the world that had not then been poisoned by antisemitism. After his success in Japan, Tokayer's work migrated to South Korea and other parts of East Asia. In the 1970s, other publishers started to publish similar books on the Talmud, including Reverend Yong-soo Hyun, who founded the Shema Education Institute, followed by Tokayer himself expanding into the South Korean market. Many of these books show more cartoons of people in front of churches than text. While there are no official English translations of these books,[15] reading one of the most popular editions of a Tokayer publication in South Korea, with the simple title *Talmud*, feels like being the last player in a game of Chinese whispers.

To summarize: after Tokayer, a native English speaker, had studied the Talmud in its Tannaitic Hebrew and Jewish Babylonian Aramaic language, his ideas about it were translated into Japanese by a later denier of Second World War war crimes and subsequently translated into Korean, which Tokayer was also not able to understand. One now faces a 'Talmud' posing such questions to the reader as 'If you were the king in this story, which of these characters would you pick for your successor?' and containing topics ranging from business ethics to sex advice to a 'Talmudic' joke from the 1930s.[16] However, Tokayer has certainly been successful at promoting his publications. There are even scholars of his work, like Meron Medzini from The Hebrew University of Jerusalem, who calls Tokayer a 'pioneer in the study of Japan and the Jews'.[17]

Journalist Ross Arbes describes the problem of having a commercialized Talmud in South Korea in his article for *The New Yorker,* where he tells of a visit to Jung Wan Kim, a PR manager and Talmud teacher, who was wearing a purple *kippah* because 'it's my branding, so that people know I am a Talmud expert'. He also tells of visiting Chul-whan Sung, then the head of the book-publishing division of Maekyung Media Group, one of the largest South Korean media companies, who estimated that 'over eighty per cent of the country' had read most of Tokayer's Talmud in some form or another.[18] While that statistic is difficult to verify, the Talmud is indeed very popular in South Korea, with almost every bookshop having copies of it. *The Jewish Chronicle* even reported that there were book-vending machines with copies of the Talmud.[19] Indeed, it is hard to find somebody in South Korea who has not at least heard of the Talmud. For example, Lee Kyou-Hyuk, who carried the South Korean flag at the 2014 Olympics, recommended the Talmud to his fans, saying, 'I read the Talmud every time I am going through a hard time. It helps me calm my mind.'[20]

Astonishingly, when searching 'Talmud' in the National Digital Library of Korea, more than 800 different books from more than 300 publishers appear, including over 160 that list Tokayer as the author. When asked how an ancient book on Jewish law can be so immensely popular in their country, most South Koreans mention the word 'wisdom'. One also gets this impression when walking along the Gangnam underground mall in Seoul, where a 'Talmud Wisdom Education School' is located across the hall from a drycleaners, the former selling a fantasy of the Jewish people and their academic accomplishments. Across from the dry cleaners is where one can meet parents like Mrs Park. This was all part of her fantasy now, too: her son learning some secret Jewish study technique, becoming wise, and eventually passing the university entry exam. I don't know if she ever awoke from this delusion, and it is hard to tell if she actually thought her son was studying anything of deep value with 'The Talmud'. But the one thing she thought for sure was that her most recent dream didn't end at least, as they so often did, in failure.

Books on the study of the Talmud itself are popular among South Koreans, too. In 2018, Salim Publishing Company in Seoul published a Korean translation of Ilana Kurshan's *If All the Seas Were Ink: A Memoir*. The book describes the author's 7-year journey studying *daf yomi*, a daily regimen of learning the Oral Torah and its commentaries where each of the 2,711 pages of the Babylonian Talmud is read, one page per day, over the course of 7 1/2 years. Samuel C. Heilman has credited the programme of *daf yomi* with making Talmud study accessible to Jews who are not Talmud scholars.[21]

With the Korean version of the 'Japanese Talmud', the Talmud is being presented to South Korean readers as a universal book of general wisdom for everybody, not only Jews. Many versions consist of aphorisms and moral lessons at the end of a story about a rabbi. These moral lessons are often quotations by Goethe, the Brothers Grimm, Aristotle, or Rilke, but could just as easily be from thinkers like Voltaire or Simone de Beauvoir. Sometimes these quotes are actually from the Talmud itself, mixing them with Western tradition, as well as Chinese or Korean sayings. An example of framing the Talmud into Chinese wisdom is a book published in 2013, *T'almudŭ Ch'aegŭndam: sesangŭl iginŭn kajang widaehan chihye* ('Talmud/Caigentan: The most powerful wisdom to win over the world'). It demonstrates how late sixteenth-century Ming dynasty philosopher Hong Zicheng's *Caigentan* ('Vegetable Roots Discourse'), with its aphorisms drawn from Confucian, Daoist, and Buddhist concepts—and which has recently become popular in South Korea—becomes infused with the Talmud.

Many Japanese Talmud are marketed to Korean Christians in particular. Versions of it often include on their cover Christian images such as churches, doves, the Evangelists, or the Virgin Mary carrying the infant Christ. Barry Scott Wimpfheimer writes in *The Talmud: A Biography* that South Koreans do believe their versions of the Talmud to be authentic, and that the Talmud is ubiquitous in Korean culture.[22] In my own experiences with South Koreans this is indeed the case. Even though the Babylonian Talmud can in a way be regarded as 'Eastern' by contemporary Jews, from a Korean perspective studying the Talmud is a way of competing with globalization and exotic Western wisdom.

Similarly, Fordham University published 'Discovering Korea Through the Talmud', an article about Sarit Kattan Gribetz and Claire Kim's research experience[23] that led to their later work 'The *Talmud* in Korea: A Study in the Reception of Rabbinic Literature'.[24] 'The *Talmud* in Korea' is a thorough study of the reception of rabbinic literature in South Korea (although not the first one, as the authors claim, but the third). The authors, unfortunately, do not fully convey the concept of philosemitism,[25] but the article describes very well the story of the 'Talmud' in Korea that 'challenges us to think about the limits of "Talmud," generically and semantically'.[26] Kattan Gribetz and Kim came to the same conclusion as Wimpfheimer, that the Talmud in Korea

is its own genre. It is not a Korean translation of the Babylonian Talmud, nor a summary or synopsis of rabbinic sources. Rather, it is a collection of traditions that originated in and was inspired by the talmudic corpus but that has taken on a textual life of its own and is best understood as a unique textual tradition currently circulating in dozens of slightly different versions ... [it] has been circulating in numerous editions since the 1970s throughout South Korea and the Korean diaspora in California, New York, and elsewhere.[27]

Interestingly, Kattan Gribetz and Kim point to a difference between the Talmud in Korea and the original when it comes to gender in the process of transmission. While the Talmud as we know it excludes women when it talks about the transmission of halakhic knowledge from father to son, in the Korean version mothers are responsible for the transmission of the rabbinic text to their sons and daughters. What this demonstrates is how the Talmud changes in the context of the traditional role of the mother in South Korean society. Kattan Gribetz and Kim argue that in South Korea a mother who teaches her children Talmud is seen as a great mother in the context of the phenomenon known as *ryōsai kenbo* (good wife, wise mother).[28]

One example of the Japanese Talmud becoming a specifically East Asian work of thought are Talmud publications for unborn children and the idea that mothers directly impact their child by exposing themselves to good readings during pregnancy. Erin M. Cline writes that 'Confucian philosophers maintain that the prenatal period, infancy, and early childhood represent a unique and irreplaceable opportunity for moral cultivation, and they offer detailed accounts of the specific role that each of these stages has'.[29] Reading to the unborn incorporates, according to Anne Kinney, 'a radical view of the environment's effect on both the spiritual and corporeal constitution of human beings. In this case, the environment is the womb, and the sensory stimuli that affect the mother simultaneously affect the fetus'.[30] The Talmud has, hence, become a way by which many South Korean mothers seek to influence the moral development of their children in accordance with Confucian ideas.

Over half of the books that are classified as 'Talmud' in the National Digital Library in South Korea are children's books. And versions of the Talmud are included on many elementary schools' suggested reading lists in South Korea. Many Koreans seem to believe that reading those books will somehow improve their children's IQ, and the very popular subgenre of the 'pre-natal Talmud' attests to the common belief that it supports brain development in the womb. Rabbi Litzman, the current Chabad rabbi in Seoul, seems fascinated by the fact that the Talmud is available in convenience stores and even in some train-station kiosks, and he proclaims that 'Koreans love Judaism.'[31]

A CASE OF PHILOSEMITISM?

But is this interest in the Talmud and Jewish education indeed a 'love' of the Jewish people? Philosemitism, or the love of Jews, is an area that has been mostly ignored by academic scholarship,[32] which comes as a surprise since it also offers a way to think about antisemitism. Only within the last decade or so have new studies on the phenomenon emerged,[33] which are important because to neglect philosemitism is to ignore one of the principal things that set Jews apart from non-Jews. The Greek prefix *philo*, 'to love', would suggest this term refers to a love of Jews, Jewishness, or what is seen to be somehow Jewish. But philosemitism is not antithetical to antisemitism because there are many instances in which philosemitism is equivalent to antisemitism, 'or is at least grounded in longstanding antisemitic assumptions, myths, and stereotypes'.[34] In cases where antisemitism passes itself as philosemitism, it can be more problematic than a more transparent antisemitism, and is what Daniel Goldhagen describes as 'antisemites in sheep's clothing'.[35] Evangelical Christian support of Zionism, for instance, often comes hand in hand with an apocalyptical theology that many consider antisemitic, as it envisions Jewish conversions during the end of days.[36]

It is, therefore, crucial to understand how these ideologies correspond to one another. They are best understood as expressions of a common tendency to treat Jews as a representation. Ultimately, philosemitism depends upon what Zygmunt Bauman called 'allosemitism': the 'practice of setting the Jews apart as a people radically different from all the others, needing separate concepts to describe and comprehend them and special treatment in all or most social intercourse'.[37] Anti-antisemitism more clearly denotes an opposition to prejudice and stereotypes related to the Jewish people, their culture, or their religion. Anti-antisemitism is what Marian Mushkat calls 'the negation of antisemitism not by sympathy to Jews but rather by understanding the negative role that antisemitism plays'.[38]

But assuming that there is a pure love toward the Jewish people that is free of antisemitism, would South Korea even be a place where this occurs? What the reports on philosemitism in South Korea misunderstand is that most Koreans are generally not interested in Judaism at all. Most South Koreans are only interested in the Talmud as a tool to educate themselves, and consequently— so they believe—to cope with globalization more satisfactorily. Hence, a real philosemitism, even if described by observers, does not exist as a widespread tendency in South Korea. There is deep admiration. But love? Perhaps one could be in love without being really interested in the other person. But, in the Korean case, there is simply a very strong interest in Jewish education, just as there is in educational thinking derived from Confucius, Pestalozzi, or others. South Koreans are overwhelmingly not interested in Jewish cooking, holidays, or history, but solely in the way Jewish people allegedly practise education.

In fact, nearly half of South Koreans do not even know about the Holocaust, while 32 per cent of those who *have* heard of it agree with the statement that 'The Holocaust happened, but the number of Jews who died in it has been greatly exaggerated by history'.[39] Overall, only 28 per cent of South Koreans both know about the Holocaust and agree that it has been accurately represented by historians. The United Nations Educational, Scientific and Cultural Organization (UNESCO) has found that the Holocaust is, if taught at all, taught without the necessary context in South Korean public schools.[40] Moreover, South Korea does not have a single Jewish museum. If one were to ask a South Korean person, 'What fascinates you about Judaism?' what would come up is Jewish success, power, and wealth, not kosher cooking, philosophy, or humour. South Koreans admire the negative stereotype of the Jews as people who figured out how to get ahead of others. The observation of Litzman and others that South Koreans 'love Judaism' is therefore a complete misconception.

A CASE OF ANTISEMITISM?

Dan Sneider of Stanford University has argued that 'The line between "Jews, aren't they incredible" and "Jews, aren't they somehow dangerous and sinister" can be pretty thin', and this is particularly the case in East Asia.[41] There certainly is a dark side to what some see as Korean philosemitism, when Jews are loved for the very same stereotypes they are hated for in other parts of the world. The myth of Jewish superior intelligence, as Sander L. Gilman points out, has its origin in the age of biological racism.[42] It is certainly a global problem, but it came to South Korea relatively recently. What Tokayer and others have done in South Korea is simply to make the Jews a brand by singling them out for greatness. While the educational industry in South Korea portrays the Jewish people very favourably, this could lead to misunderstandings and expectations that cannot be fulfilled by Jews. Nor can it be achieved by Koreans, who seek to crack the code of some imaginary secret learning technique that Jews allegedly practise. Koreans might not only become disappointed when studying what they believe to be the Talmud does not lead them to the most amazing success, but the stereotype might even lead them to the dangerous belief that Jews are taking advantage of these special powers and wisdom that they themselves would like to have. This might especially come to pass in a country like South Korea, where Jews are abstractions in people's minds without any real historical presence in the country.

In fact, this problem can already be seen in a 2014 survey conducted by the Anti-Defamation League (ADL), where more than half of South Koreans agreed with the statements that 'Jews have too much power in the business world', 'Jews have too much control over the global media', and 'Jews have too much control over global affairs'. Ultimately, 'More than half of the adult population of South Korea, about 53 percent, agreed with a majority of 11 classical stereotypes about Jews'.[43] While the

ADL understood its findings as demonstrating South Korean antisemitism, Dave Hazzan argued in *Tablet* that those same sentiments reflected Korean philosemitism.[44] Controlling the world's business and political affairs would be something Koreans aspired to. Rabbi Litzman argues in the same way in *Tablet,* stating:

> Everything [in the ADL survey] was about 'too much'. What can you answer when everyone is asking about 'too much'? If you say 'no,' what do you mean, it's too *little*? The questions were not clear for Koreans. For them, 'too much' means 'a lot'. So, what's wrong with it? There's nothing wrong with it. They admire this and they want to be the same. One of the questions was, 'Do the Jews control the media too much?' or something like that ... They look at it as a model.[45]

The ADL leadership has certainly become 'a lightning rod for vicious criticism from both the left and the right'[46] in recent years, and not entirely without a reason. Yet, one should distinguish here between the poor quality of certain leadership decisions in terms of public advocacy, and ADL's interesting polling work, which despite its flaws points to something important. At least media reports seem to confirm its findings regarding South Korea. *The Times of Israel* reported, for example, that Jae-Seon Park, the former South Korean Ambassador to Morocco, said about Jews that: 'They are grabbing the currency markets and financial investment companies' and 'Their network is tight knit beyond one's imagination.' The day after Park made this statement, YTN, a Korean news and current events cable channel, quoted an economic researcher, Bag-Nee Kim, as saying: 'It is a fact that Jews use financial networks and have influence wherever they are born.'[47]

In 2015, a Samsung subsidiary removed online cartoons that depicted Paul Singer, the Jewish founder of a hedge fund, as a vulture with a large beak, but only after the cartoons had been displayed on the company's website for several weeks. The Samsung Group is South Korea's largest family-controlled conglomerate and is among the biggest employers in the country. At least two South Korean media outlets blamed Jews for attempting to block a deal

Samsung had tried to make.[48] South Korean financial publication *Money Today* wrote:

> According to the finance industry, the fact that Elliott [a hedge fund] and ISS [an advisory firm that analyzed the merger] are both Jewish institutions cannot be ignored. Elliott is led by a Jew, Paul E. Singer, and ISS is an affiliate of Morgan Stanley Capital International (MSCI), whose key shareholders are Jewish. According to a source in the finance industry, Jews have a robust network demonstrating influence in a number of domains.[49]

Meanwhile, *Mediapen*, another South Korean publication, published that 'Jews are known to wield enormous power on Wall Street and in global financial circles', and it is a 'well-known fact that the US government is swayed by Jewish capital'. Jewish money, it reported, 'has long been known to be ruthless and merciless'.[50] The ADL responded: 'Sadly, this controversy reflects the attitudes in our polling results. Antisemitism is a concern in South Korea and the government needs to publicly condemn these ugly expressions and educate people as to why these stereotypes are dangerous and false.'[51] What also comes to mind in this regard is the notorious Korean Unification Church of Sun Myung Moon, whose followers are referred to as 'Moonies' by some people. The Unification Church proclaimed that Jews had lost their status as the chosen people since the new Messiah, Sun Myung Moon, was born in Korea.[52] Moon himself has also made some terrible statements about the Holocaust, including that its Jewish victims were paying indemnity for the crucifixion of Jesus.[53]

Scholar of Korean studies Konstantin Asmolov has made the argument that many people in South Korea don't know anything about the Jewish people except for those who they may have read about in the Bible, considering that South Koreans are about 28 per cent Christian. 'So it is possible that when answering the [ADL] survey, some respondents were guided by what the prophets said about the people of Israel.'[54] But even if that analysis is true, that is often exactly what makes an antisemite, a person who has never encountered any Jews but has strong opinions about them due to some ideology or religious text like the Bible. Following Asmolov's argument, almost any antisemitism could be naïvely justified.

In fact, what is so puzzling is South Korea's seeming lack of outrage at the commercialization and trivialization of the Holocaust, even though Koreans still feel anger toward Japan for the Second World War. Very few make the moral jump from deploring Japan's war crimes in Korea to feeling empathy with Hitler's victims, according to Cho Hae Jung, an anthropologist at Yonsei University.[55] For instance, there used to be an 'Adolf Hitler Techno Bar & Cocktail Show' in the South Korean city of Busan. After criticism, it was renamed to 'Ddolf Ditler Techno Bar & Cocktail Show.' In Seoul, a bar called 'Third Reich', which was decorated in Nazi style, changed its name to 'Fifth Reich' after protests from the German and Israeli embassies, until it finally shut down. Another bar in Seoul advertised with a poster showing a man dressed in a Nazi uniform doing a Hitler salute. *Time* magazine reported that 'the owner denies it ever had a Nazi theme. The ads, he says, must have been put up by a waiter who called himself Hitler'.[56]

On South Korean TV, an advertisement by a big Korean confectioner featured one of Korea's most popular comedians as an angry Hitler who, after taking a bite, has his mood improve. The ad campaign was stopped after the Simon Wiesenthal Center protested to Korean diplomats in the United States. In addition, the Seoul subway used to carry an ad for a popular online community that showed a man dressed in leather Nazi garb with the slogan: 'We just want masters.'[57]

RACISM IN SOUTH KOREA

While antisemitism in South Korea has been gauged as being present in more than half (i.e., 53 per cent) of the population, it has been calculated as being present in 23 per cent of the population in Japan, 20 per cent in the People's Republic of China, and at just 3 per cent in the Philippines. South Korea is, thus, similar to Iran (56 per cent) vis-à-vis the presence of antisemitism.[58] This fact should not be minimized but, rather, interpreted in the context of a more general trend towards racism and xenophobia in South Korea. According to a 2010–14 World Values Survey, 44.2 per cent of South Koreans reported they would not want a foreigner as a neighbour.[59] A 2000 survey showed that 93 per cent of South Koreans believe their nation to be comprised of a shared common bloodline.[60] And a 2016 BBC poll of several different countries found that South Korea had the highest percentage of people who stated that race was the most important factor defining national identity.[61]

Related discrimination has also been reported with regards to mixed-race children. It was only in 2011 that South Korea abandoned a regulation barring mixed-race men from enlisting in the military, also changing the oath of enlistment from referencing racial purity (*minjok*)[62] to the more inclusive reference to being Korean by nationality. *Minjok* concepts have been withdrawn from school curricula as well due to international pressure, especially from the UN Committee on the Elimination of Racial Discrimination. The UN has further complained about persistent ethnic-centric thinking in South Korea that 'might be an obstacle to the realization of equal treatment and respect for foreigners and people belonging to different races and cultures'.[63]

South Korean nationalism is quite different from the sense of patriotism characterized by loyalty towards the state that other nations feel. While identification with the Korean race is strong, that with the Republic of Korea is rather weak. Some scholars argue that Koreans (in both the North and the South) tend to ascribe to the myth that, of all the peoples in the world, they are the least inclined to premeditated evil, something Brian R. Myers describes in his brilliant study on North Korea as the feeling of belonging to the 'cleanest race'.[64] John W. Dower describes this belief system of moral superiority among many Japanese and Koreans during the Second World War, as well.[65]

A Korean national identification with Jews becomes apparent when reading the independence activist Ahn Chang Ho, who wrote in 1907: 'Christ told the Jews that it was because they were full of evil deeds and devoid of all goodness that God took their rights from them and handed them over to others, and this surely applies to Korea today.'[66] This illuminates the psychological confusion many Koreans feel in the face of modernization, and the various ways that they identify with Jews help them to resolve it.

As South Korea modernized over the 1980s through 2010, it adopted many Western ideas about the Jews. Coming to terms with 'the Jews' became a way to come to terms with modernity and the West, or of being able to reject it. In this struggle to find a place in the modern world, Koreans might identify themselves with Jews while simultaneously rejecting them. In this sense, Korean philosemitism and antisemitism are not opposites but are both expressions of an underlying struggle for self-construction in the modern world. Each of these two phenomena reveals how individuals cope with the challenges of globalization in situations like those that presently exist in South Korea.

But to believe that South Koreans 'love the Jews', despite the major problems of racism and xenophobia that one finds in South Korea—as if the Jews were somehow the only people left off the traditional hate list in this instance, and by those who have often expressed a strong dislike for others—is extremely naïve. It would certainly be the first time such a turn of events has occurred, given that Jews are normally the very first target of bigotry and prejudice. It seems much more likely that the Anti-Defamation League survey, with its finding that 53 per cent of Koreans hold strong antisemitic attitudes, is correct and in line with findings on the presence of xenophobia more generally in South Korea. Both of these attitudes result from the pressures of globalization on a rapidly changing and deeply unhappy country.

HELL JOSEON

South Korea, like many countries, faces a situation of educational inflation where many highly educated—some might say over educated—students want to work for South Korea's biggest conglomerates, or *chaebols*, such as Samsung and LG Electronics. However, in spite of their best efforts (and the efforts of tiger moms like Mrs Park), most graduates find themselves unable to find jobs that match their level of education. The problem, especially in

South Korea, is that those who are unsuccessful in this competition for the best jobs become somewhat second-class citizens, with fewer opportunities for employment and even marriage. The consequence is that depression and suicide, anger and frustration, are all on the rise in Korean society. Young Koreans have come up with a satirical term for this, using a historic name for a Korean kingdom: 'Hell Joseon'. The term circulated first online but has rapidly been adapted by mass media and a generation of South Koreans who equate the high levels of social inequality in their country with living in hell. In this case, they use the term 'Joseon' instead of 'Korea' in reference to a period (1392–1910) when the country was ruled by a small elite while the rest of the population was stuck in poverty.

Apart from the satirical drawing of parallels, South Korea is increasingly heading towards becoming an extremely unequal and unstable society, where wealth is concentrated among the *chaebol* and younger people are less and less likely to find fulfilling employment, if any at all. Part of that frustration over the false promise the South Korean education system has made will, I fear, turn into criticism of the Talmud and 'Jewish education'. This might not automatically lead to more antisemitism, but it certainly is a problem which needs to be addressed.

Some of my colleagues in South Korea have pointed to the fact that antisemitism in their country cannot be a major problem due to the very small number of Jews living in South Korea, most of whom are not even in the country permanently. But that only means that antisemitism in South Korea is not a problem for the Jewish people themselves, and it assumes that such negative attitudes do not affect South Korea as a country and society as a whole. The existence of antisemitism is always a sign of social and cultural failure, indeed, of a diminishing capacity to understand the modern world, let alone to thrive in it. It is not a Jewish problem as much as it is a problem for South Korea's culture and economic future. As Walter Russel Mead has put it so well:

> People who think 'the Jews' run the banks lose the ability to understand, much less to operate financial systems. People who

think 'the Jews' dominate business through hidden structures can't build or long maintain a successful modern economy. People who think 'the Jews' dominate politics lose their ability to interpret political events, to diagnose social evils and to organize effectively for positive change. People who think 'the Jews' run the media and control the news lose the ability to grasp what is happening around them.[67]

Moreover, people who think 'the Jews' control US foreign policy lose the ability to understand, much less to influence it. Many South Koreans, overwhelmed by modernization, are seduced by empty and grotesque generalizations about the Jewish people being smarter and more powerful than other humans. This view, a collective myth which many Koreans have formed about a group of people they have almost never encountered, does not actually help to explain a faster and more confusing world. What South Korea needs is emancipation from the idea that the Jewish people are in any way different from other human beings. Only then will it be able to act effectively and meaningfully in today's world.

A good starting point for beginning to fix this problem would be the South Korean educational system, which seems rather broken. With its rote memorizations and lack of any emphasis on analytical thinking, it runs a high risk of creating further stereotypes about Jews. Thinking analytically and creating a world view that harmonizes with the facts surrounding us, rather than simply memorizing ideas, is certainly a hard task for anyone, Korean or not. But, as Koreans say, 'Go-saeng Ggeut-eh naki eun-da—at the end of hardship comes happiness.' And more happiness is what South Korea certainly needs.

2

LONELINESS AND THE SYMBOLIC
VIEW OF JEWS IN JAPAN[1]

Mayumi Asai[2] remembers the first time she had ramen in public all by herself. She was in college, and back then it was rather unusual in Japan for a woman to eat ramen alone. She entered the restaurant nervously, as she felt she was doing something differently from others who went out to eat in pairs and groups. She thought she was doing something wrong. But Japan, a country where conformity is highly valued, has changed greatly since then. More than a third of its households contain only one person, and by 2040 it is estimated that this number will increase to nearly 40 per cent. And *ohitorisama*—doing things alone—has gained popularity in Japan, with surveys indicating that younger people even value time alone over time spent with family members or friends. People like Mayumi Asai might even find it more enjoyable to go to karaoke alone, or for drinks after work not with their colleagues but all by themselves. Of course, this makes it even harder to understand social attitudes in Japan, a country that has puzzled social scientists from abroad for generations.

UNDERSTANDING JAPAN

Matthew Perry, who in 1854 forced Japan to reopen its ports to the world after over 200 years, complained about Japanese people not voicing their opinions enough. A journal entry of his notes: 'Notwithstanding that the Japanese are themselves so fond of indulging their curiosity, they are by no means communicative when information is required of them ... It was evident that nothing but fear of punishment deterred them from entering into free intercourse with us.'[3]

In this context, one finds in post-Second World War Japan a distinction between two important concepts: *honne* ('true sound') are one's true feelings, as opposed to *tatemae* ('built in front'), the opinion a person displays in public.[4] *Honne* is often kept hidden in Japan, in case it stands against society's expectations, and this can lead to outright lies when it comes to expressing one's thoughts. The *honne–tatemae* divide is considered by some scholars to be highly important to understanding Japanese society,[5] and it certainly makes research on the ideas of the Japanese regarding the Jewish people quite difficult. But, of course, this is not a uniquely Japanese phenomenon. In Western societies, too, if someone asks one 'do I look good in this outfit?' or 'am I beautiful?', one would be expected—if the answer is 'no'—to lie to them.

Another issue that may prevent the Japanese from voicing their real opinion is the importance of situational awareness, which is certainly a valuable skill in any culture. But in Japan, with its often rather indirect form of communication, *kuuki o yomu*—reading the air—becomes an ever-present consideration. Misreading the air can potentially end friendships, relationships, or business deals. In 2019, a Japanese businessman's tweet went viral in Japan when he reflected back on a business meeting he had in Kyoto, during which a potential client complimented him: 'That's a really nice watch you've got.'[6] So the businessman started to talk about the watch's various features, only to regret it in hindsight. Not because it made him appear to be too materialistic or showing off, but because he eventually realized that his client wasn't really complimenting him on his watch, but rather wanted him to look down on it to see what time it was, and thus come to the conclusion that the conversation had gone on for much too long.

'Reading the air' requires, according to Yoko Hasegawa, Professor of Japanese Linguistics at the University of California, Berkeley, not only cultural and historical knowledge but also knowledge of those involved in a conversation. If two people, for instance, 'are praising each other, it might be the case that they are arch-enemies. If you can't read this "air", you might say something that inflames the hostile relationship'.[7] For a Japanese person to praise 'Jewish wisdom' or 'wealth' might, hence, not necessarily mean they are expressing admiration, but rather must be seen in context. Those who are 'unable to read the air' are referred to by the pejorative slang term 'KY', which stands for *kuuki ga yomenai*: someone who doesn't realize that a guest wants another cup of tea, or who speaks on their mobile phone on a train, that sort of behaviour. According to Japanese social psychologist Shinobu Kitayama, 'Often times, you'll be kicked out from important discussions in many organisations. And sometimes, that [KY] can be part of the reason for school bullying.'[8] Hence, Yoko Hasegawa recommends that one 'cultivate the desire to behave like others'[9] in Japan.

Scholars trying to understand Japan have often pointed out the country's unique culture. Cultural differences between Japan and the rest of the world have even made some scholars suggest that Japan is impossible to research and theorize about. American economist Chalmers Johnson argues that Western economic theories are incapable of adequately explaining Japan's economic achievements:

> still the people who play a leading role in this field, rather argue that Japan is an exception ('cultural peculiarity' is their excuse), than conclude that this failure is a question of economic theory or they (by juggling the figures) forcibly change the Japanese data to fit in with the theory.[10]

The argument that Japan is a unique case that stands apart from the rest of the world due to the country consisting of islands and having a long history of isolation, has been expressed beyond the field of economics. The idea of Japanese uniqueness, or *nihonjinron*[11] ('theories of Japaneseness' or 'discussion of the Japanese'),[12] is a common genre of thought in Japan itself.[13] It consists of all kinds of themes, from 'race' to social structure or cultural origins.[14] 'Essentially, the message ... is that Japan, the Japanese, and Japanese society are unique in the world—topographically, linguistically, structurally, culturally, even anatomically.'[15] *Nihonjinron* 'often leads [Japanese people] to believe that foreigners will never be able to learn the Japanese language and that they will never really understand the Japanese culture'.[16] Harumi Befu observes the problem well: '*Nihonjinron* ... aims to demonstrate the superiority of Japanese culture over other cultures.'[17] But *nihonjinron* is not valid, nor does it serve Japan itself particularly well. During the Second World War, 'the Japanese military, at one point, transmitted messages uncoded under the delusion that the Allies would be unable to understand Japanese'.[18] In fact, the idea of the Japanese language being particularly unique is far from true. It might appear that way from an English-language point of view, since English follows a subject-verb-object sentence structure, yet Japanese, with its subject-object-verb structure,[19] is among the world's most frequently occurring language types.[20] Similarly, Ray T. Donahue also tells how 'some Japanese school children assume that the metric system, which Japan follows, must be unique because English measurement is (or was) non-metrical'.[21]

Interestingly, 'Westerners teach their children to communicate their ideas clearly and to adopt a "transmitter" orientation, that is, the speaker is responsible for uttering sentences that can be clearly understood by the hearer—and understood, in fact, more or less independently of the context,' explains Richard E. Nisbett. 'It's the speaker's fault if there is a miscommunication. Asians, in contrast, teach their children a 'receiver' orientation, meaning that it is the hearer's responsibility to understand what is being said.'[22] For example, 'If a child's loud singing annoys an American parent, the parent would be likely just to tell the kid to pipe down. No ambiguity there.'[23] An Asian parent, on the other hand, 'would be more likely to say, 'How well you sing a song.' At first the child might feel pleased, but it would likely dawn on the child that something else might have been meant and the child would try being quieter or not singing at all'.[24] Consequently, Westerners are likely to find East Asians hard to read, while the latter most likely assume that they have made their point indirectly clear. On the other hand, people at the Eastern end of Asia are likely to find Westerners too direct and perhaps even rude. One therefore needs to take into consideration that, in East Asia, an antisemitic statement could also be meant to refer to a context that is not related to Jews at all.

But, of course, Japan can and should be studied and theorized. And by no means do the cultural differences between Japan and an outside observer mean that it is impossible to understand the country. Opinion polls, for instance, do work very well in Japan. In fact, Japan has been described as one of the major countries for public opinion polling,[25] and one can draw considerable knowledge from them as they filter out those cultural obstacles that prevent people from voicing their *honne*, their true opinion.

PHILO- AND ANTISEMITISM IN JAPAN

Understanding Japan is rather complicated when it comes to concepts that don't exist in the country. 'Nature' is one example of this, since the Japanese had, strictly speaking, 'no concept of Nature as such prior to their contact with Western culture',[26] and even today Westerners talking about 'nature' with Japanese people may run into misunderstandings. It can be equally confusing when surveys ask about something as foreign to the Japanese as 'Jews'. Surveys, however, seem to provide a rather clear picture: antisemitism is a problem in Japan. The 2014 Anti-Defamation League poll found 23 per cent of Japanese to be antisemites,[27] which adds up to about 25 million people. This problem exists despite the country not having any significant Jewish presence or history.[28]

The phenomenon often leads to confusion on the part of scholars of antisemitism. *Anti-Semitism and Psychiatry* by H. Steven Moffic et al. states, for instance, that 'Anti-semitism can arise even in regions where Jews are absent, as was the case in Japan during the 1820s and 1830s, when the Japanese expressed hostile views of Jews even though they had never met one.'[29] This is, however, not quite possible, as Japan was cut off from the world until 1853. In fact, as stated in the introduction, antisemitism came to Japan through the Japanese versions of *The Merchant of Venice* and *the Protocols of the Elders of Zion*.[30] According to Tom Brislin, who studies contemporary Japan, 'Anti-Semitic books and articles are not uncommon in Japan. Most tend to favor conspiracy theories of international Jewish control of political and economic forces, and attempts to subdue the Japanese economy.'[31] He further reports that two months before the 1995 attack on Tokyo's subway by the Aum Shinrikyo sect using

> Nazi-developed sarin poison gas, a leading Japanese news magazine published a story 'There Were No Nazi Gas Chambers!' in World War II. Ironically, large ads for the Holocaust-denial article hung in hundreds of subway cars throughout Tokyo's myriad mass transit system. The magazine, *Marco Polo*, was on sale at numerous newsstands in the cavernous Kasumigaseki station, the gassing target where three major subway lines meet and thousands of officials and workers disembark beneath the metropolitan government complex.[32]

Since the mid-1980s, whole sections of bookshops around Japan contain books about *Yudayajin* (Jewish people) with titles such as *The Secret of Jewish Power That Moves the World* and *The Jewish Plot to Control the World*. According to Brislin, 'The anti-Semitic tone of such books, educators, authors and officials believe, is borne not so much out of hatred as out of ignorance and economic uncertainty.'[33] Japanese historian Sachiko Sakamaki believes that 'The Japanese don't know anything about the Jews. That's why they imagine things.'[34] Tellingly, Israeli diplomat Arie Dan recollects his graduate study in Business Administration at Japan's prestigious Keio University: 'In my classes, my own professors, learned men, would espouse international Jewish conspiracy theories to control the Japanese Economy.'[35]

In 1993, two popular journals, the *Nihon Keizai (Nikkei) Shimbun* and *Shukan Bunshun*, printed advertisements for 'Get Japan, the Last Enemy: The Jewish Protocols for World Domination', described by Goodman and Miyazawa as:

> Emblazoned with Jewish stars and an image of Satan, the ad claimed that 'Jewish cartels surrounding the Rothschilds control Europe, America, and Russia and have now set out to conquer Japan!' It outlined the Jewish scenario to destroy the Japanese economy, blaming the Jews for everything from the cut in Japanese interest rates in 1987 to the Gulf War and predicting the 'reoccupation' of Japan by Jews by the end of the decade.[36]

However, 'The anti-Semitic success phenomenon is not restricted to relatively unknown authors boosted to fame through media advertisement and coverage.'[37] Eisaburo Saito, a member of the Upper House of the Japanese Diet, wrote *The Secret of Jewish Power to Control the World*, and a book by Yoshio Ogai, an influential official of Japan's Liberal Democratic Party, 'prescribes Hitler as a role model for winning office in *Hitler Election Strategy: A Bible for Certain Victory in Modern Elections*'.[38] The Buddhist nationalist Tanaka Chigaku even ran an antisemitic campaign for the Lower House of Parliament in 1924,[39] and Buddhist thinkers such as D.T. Suzuki and Hakuun Yasutani have promoted antisemitism.[40] In 2014, the national daily *Sankei Shimbun* published advertisements for a book which claimed that the United States is a 'Jewish dictatorship' and that the devastating earthquake and tsunami of March 2011 were a Jewish conspiracy.[41]

Antisemitism often occurs in countries that struggle to tackle racism in general. Japan understands itself as 'a society predicated upon the rule of law' (*hō no shihai suru shakai, hōchi kokka*).[42] Racial discrimination is unconstitutional in Japan (Article 14), but, as confusing as it may sound—and despite much international criticism[43]—it is not illegal. On the contrary, racism is commonly seen in the form of landlords refusing to rent an apartment to a foreigner, or restaurants and hotels refusing non-local customers (*gaikokujin okotowari*).[44] In 2006, the Setaka Town Assembly in Southern Japan passed a resolution 'granting permission to build a new university in town, but only if it had no exchange students (*ryūgakusei*). The reported reason given was a fear of "foreign crime" that foreign students might cause'.[45] In 2015, Sono Ayako, novelist and former advisor on education reform to Prime Minister Abe Shinzō, advocated for racial segregation in the daily newspaper *Sankei Shimbun*: 'Since learning about the situation in South Africa 20 or 30 years ago, I've come to think that whites, Asians and blacks should live separately.'[46] Other things are not as easy to put into categories. It is, for instance, quite common in Japan to be asked at job interviews or social interactions what blood type one is.

It is noteworthy in this context to add that no university in Japan has established a department for Jewish (or Israel) Studies. Unfortunately, we are faced with a lack of scholars educating the Japanese public with their work.[47] In my personal experience in Japan, even some academics believe to some degree in antisemitic stereotypes. Shichihei Yamamoto's 1971 bestseller *The Japanese and the Jews* (*Nihonjin to Yudayajin*) was one of three antisemitic books I found on my desk the first day of my visiting faculty post at a Japanese university. Written under the pseudonym 'Isaiah Ben-Dasan', the book won the second Ōya Prize for Nonfiction. Yamamoto makes the claim that Jews are 'skilful, cautious handlers of money',[48] 'nomads', and responsible for the Holocaust.[49] Handing me these books from the university library was not an act of hostility, so I believe, but rather a friendly gesture of a colleague leaving me books that might interest me.

In order to fully understand the concept of Jewish people as they exist in the imaginations of many Japanese, one must also understand positive, philosemitic ideas that circulate in Japan. These ideas are poised to become stronger and more widespread, given Japan's sociopsychological situation where more and more people face a loneliness that fosters stereotypical thinking—like antisemitism and philosemitism—without Jews even having any significant presence in the country itself. The Japanese fascination with Judaism comes as a surprise, given the differences between both cultures. And Jews constitute only about 0.0002 per cent of the population in Japan, most of them foreigners and short-term residents.

Unfortunately, most Japanese show little interest in Jewish institutions such as the communities in Tokyo and Kobe, which, for their part, do little to nothing to establish a dialogue with local Japanese people, instead seeing themselves as expat communities. Establishing Jewish studies programmes outside North America and Europe in countries such as Japan would certainly help to change the root of the problem of antisemitism which, in Japan, derives from academic thinking or fantasizing due to a lack of knowledge. One would do well not to overlook this part of the world any longer, and to encourage the Jewish communities in Japan to maintain links with Japanese scholars and the public, especially since the few scholars of Old Testament studies in Japan, too, would certainly benefit from an exchange.[50]

THE LINE BETWEEN PHILOSEMITISM AND ANTISEMITISM IN JAPAN

In Japan, Jews are seen as different not only from the Japanese but from other Westerners, which sets them further apart. Yet Jews have played a role in modern Japanese history without being present. The best example of this is Jacob Schiff, an American Jewish banker who, during the Russo-Japanese war, arranged two big loans that helped Japan avoid financial collapse.[51] The Japanese reaction to Schiff can be seen as an example of the fusion between antisemitism and philosemitism in the country. He was honoured by the emperor of Japan and toasted when he visited in 1906. At the same time, he was viewed as the best example of Jewish international power. In the case of Schiff, problematic stereotypical fantasies of the Jewish people in general were combined in forms of philosemitic admiration and antisemitic hate.

In this context, one can also cite a plan, which was ultimately not realized, by some Japanese officials in the early 1930s to bring 50,000 German Jews fleeing from the Nazis to settle them in occupied Manchuria in order to use their capital and expertise to develop the region.[52] In the late 1930s, the Japanese authorities in Manchuria established the Far Eastern Jewish Congress with the idea of controlling the Jews in East Asia and using them to communicate with, and influence, the Roosevelt administration in the United States,[53] a plan that eventually failed.

One might be inclined to assume that philosemitism affects antisemitism and vice versa in Japan as it does in other countries. Yet Japan is different. The Japanese political scientist Masao Maruyama has convincingly demonstrated in his book *Nihon no Shisō (Japanese Thought)*[54] how various indigenous, as well as foreign, ideas and concepts exist in Japan in a way in which everything is kept and expressed in the form in which it was initially received. According to Maruyama, in Japan an idea's validity is never tested against another, and there is no hybridizing of concepts. There are many terms for the word 'I' in Japanese (*watakushi*, *boku*, *ore*, and so on) dependent on the circumstance, the person speaking, and the person being addressed. 'In this respect,' psychologist Hayao Kawai who served as director of the International Research Center for Japanese Studies wrote, 'it can be said that the Japanese finds "I" solely through the existence of others. However, if this aspect is over-emphasised, one might conclude that the Japanese are so passive as to accept everything that comes their way and that they have no autonomy. The actual situation is more subtle.'[55] In Japan, it is possible for someone to host uncombined philosophies and concepts: every concept is kept and expressed in the form it was initially received,[56] and in their mind one typically does not mix philosemitism with antisemitism as much as might be expected in a non-Japanese context. Yet, the paradox of philo- and antisemitism existing side by side has struck scholars of Japan, such as Brislin:

> As is typical of conspiracy theories, the *Yudayajin* conspiracism in Japanese publishing targets no particular Jews as the heads or organizers of the feared cabal. Only their agents, ranging from the U.S. President to pop diva Madonna, are attacked, under the premise that their actions are controlled by shadowy puppeteers in the world domination market ... Conversely, the accomplishments of actual, individual Jews whether in the arena of finance or war are portrayed as heroic and admirable.[57]

Another example would be the prestigious Bungei Shunjū publishing company. The company simultaneously published *Anne Frank's Diary* but also, on the day of the fiftieth anniversary of the liberation of Auschwitz, published the 'There Were No Nazi "Gas Chambers"' article via its monthly magazine *Marco Polo*.[58]

The tendency in Japan to avoid challenging ideas against one another can also be seen in the area of religion. Contrary to the Western idea of adhering to a single religion, a Japanese person may visit a Shinto shrine on New Year's, follow Buddhist temple rituals, and have a Christian-style wedding ceremony without feeling the need to test these religions against one another. The history of places of worship of Buddhism as well as *kami* (known later as a part of Shinto) testified to this mindset until the Meiji Restoration under the influence of the West separated both.[59] Japan has, in this regard, something valuable to teach: that religious freedom, it could be argued, only exists in such a setting, just as freedom of thought only exists if one is allowed to have contrary viewpoints at the same time.

THE CONCEPT OF THE STRANGER IN JAPANESE CULTURE

Japanese attitudes to Jews and foreigners in general are deeply rooted in Japanese culture. Even before they were aware of the existence of the Jewish people, the Japanese had certain ways of relating to foreigners that 'conditioned the way they would eventually conceive Jews in the imagination'.[60] Teigo Yoshida speaks of symbolic aspects of the notion of 'stranger' he found in traditional Japan:

> The Portuguese who came to Japan during the sixteenth century were considered to have come from 'tenjiku' and were referred to as the tenjiku-jin (people of tenjiku). Tenjiku ... denotes a remote place, a mountain peak, the sky, and a foreign country. It was believed then that Europeans came to Japan from such a distant place. Obviously, the people of tenjiku were associated with supernatural power in the minds of most Japanese of the day. For example, Francisco Xavier, a Spanish Jesuit missionary, was once walking in heavy snow in some mountainous region when he met a Japanese who requested that he, 'a man from tenjiku,' reduce the amount of snowfall.[61]

According to historical documents, during the sixteenth century many Japanese believed newly introduced Christianity to be a religion of black magic and witchcraft, and that Christians could make grass and trees wither just by touching them.[62] Even later, in 1853, when Commodore Matthew Perry came to Japan with his steam-powered ships, forcing regular trade and exchange between Japan and the outside world for the first time in over 200 years, many Japanese were frightened by the perceived mystical powers of the foreign visitors. According to documents written in that period, some believed that 'magical' Americans could find personal treasures.[63] The tale of magic-endowed foreigners capable of finding mystical stones and other materials was essential to Japanese culture, shifting from the Chinese to European missionaries from Portugal and Spain to the Americans,[64] and ultimately to the Jewish people, who are seen as being mystically successful in business. Japanese historian Yokoyama Toshio describes an unconscious tendency among many Japanese to put Westerners 'on a pedestal, almost to the point of thinking of them as supernatural beings, even gods'.[65]

Foreigners and other strangers were historically regarded as being potentially dangerous, but could also be credited for being the reason for one's good fortune.[66] This ambivalence between threat and awe of the *marebito*, the visitors from afar, has been significant in Japanese culture and religious life. 'Secularized and aestheticized, it became the foundation of traditional Japanese theatre forms like Nō and Kabuki; and its influence continues to be felt in Japanese culture today.'[67] This mix of annoyance, apprehension, and admiration has often been described as a 'foreigner complex' (*gaijin konpurekkusu*).[68] The Japanese have followed this pattern of both idealization and demonization in their perception of Jews, viewing them as visitors from far away who are a potential threat and, at the same time, could bring good fortunes.

Before the opening up of Japan in 1853, the country was suffering a spiritual crisis from within: Buddhism, which had governed Japanese religious life for centuries, had been in such decline that some expected it to vanish completely from Japan within a few years.[69] Neo-Confucianism was seen as too rationalistic, and Christianity had been the target of attacks since the 1630s.[70] Only what we describe today as Shinto was rising in influence, while numerous new healing cults and messianic religions (*shinkō shūkyō*) emerged during the early nineteenth century in Japan as a response to a perceived spiritual chaos.[71] The forced opening up of the country after 200 years of isolation only intensified this struggle. The continuing driving force of Japanese history is a sense of an imminent moral collapse, and xenophobia is in part a defence mechanism, using real and imagined threats from the outside to ultimately vitalize Japanese spirituality and identity. The response to Japan's internal crisis is the foundation of contemporary xenophobia and antisemitism in the country,[72] but it is also the ground from which a fantasy of the Jewish people as the strangers bringing good fortune emerged. Ironically, antisemitic writer Uno Masami wasn't far off, at least with the title of his terrible bestseller *If You Understand the Jews, You Will Understand the Japanese.*[73] By understanding how Japanese view the Jewish people, one can learn much about the way Japanese think of the world they live in.

MODERN ISOLATION IN JAPAN

Unfortunately, the spiritual and social crisis continues in today's Japan. Masao Maruyama argued that the unprecedented openness that accompanied Japan's modernization often went hand-in-hand with an increasing tendency for images to convey perceptions of reality.[74] These images often become fixed and standardized as stereotypes, which narrow down perception. This tendency is, of course, driven by the specialization of knowledge and compartmentalization. When a traditional society, such as Japan's, opens up to the 'free and rapid flow of information [it] ironically results in new forms of closedness'.[75] Ishihara Shintaro, before becoming governor of Tokyo, argued together with then chairman of Sony, Morita Akio, that Japan's intercultural communication must change in that the Japanese 'must move out of their current mental stagnation' by being comfortable outside their homes and family. In their view, this was particularly important for Japanese diplomats: 'Except for the young and especially qualified, most Japanese diplomats suffer from a peculiar inferiority complex [and] as a result are spreading the seeds of misunderstanding throughout the world.'[76]

In Japan, groups tend to be *marugakae*, to act loyally to the group's way of thinking. Adding this specific feature of Japanese society to the global tendency of specializing the consumption of information results in what Maruyama calls an 'octopus pot society' (*takotsubo shakai*), in which 'self-contained groups rely on their own sources of information, display paranoid reactions toward outsiders, and refuse to engage in the open discussion and debate that are fundamental to modern civil society'.[77] (This is an important development for the study of antisemitism in general, as the West has become very much like this, too.)

This problem is especially crucial when a society becomes more and more lonely on top of it, with people like Mayumi Asai increasingly doing everything in their life all alone, not just eating ramen. A term that describes contemporary Japan well is *otaku*. Literally meaning 'one's home', the term was originally used in the eighties as slang for young adults who shied away from traditional relationships in favour of the fantasy worlds of videogames, anime, and manga. Academics at first had a hard time understanding a generation's refusal to leave behind the entertainments of youth and embrace adulthood, and the *otaku*'s childish lifestyle became something of a societal embarrassment which the public and media alike ignored. In Japanese media they are often described as 'parasite singles' and 'herbivore men'. But by the second decade of the twenty-first century most people, Japanese and Westerners alike, have adopted an *otaku* lifestyle to some extent: spending more and more time in front of screens, becoming more and more sexually inactive,[78] being less likely to move out their parents' home,[79] and obsessing over their virtual identities and infantile pleasures—from the most perfect cupcakes to the latest videogame—while having a harder time understanding the world around us. But understanding the world around them is crucial for not falling into the mental abyss of antisemitism.

In 2001, sci-fi author William Gibson—the writer who coined the phrase 'cyberspace'—interestingly wrote that 'Japan is the global imagination's default setting for the future',[80] and that 'the Japanese seem to the rest of us to live several measurable clicks down the time line'.[81] What Gibson had in mind were robot sushi bars and products like high-tech cellphones. But what he failed to see was that not only were Japanese consumer goods showing a glimpse of the future of the West, but Japanese societal trends as well: economic stagnation, the collapse of social safety nets such as the promise of lifetime employment, high rates of unemployment, high debt, political dysfunction, a sinking birth rate, an aging population (adult diapers outsell baby diapers in Japan), and the postponements of milestones of adulthood (or at least what society has understood them to be for previous generations), such as getting married or moving out of the family home.

These days, the Western world has become increasingly like Japan: younger people are losing the ambition, or ability to acquire outward expressions of wealth, status, or economic stability, and shifting instead towards a post-materialist 'experience economy',[82] where personal fulfillment—including activities such as eating out, travelling, and other leisure experiences driving the economy—becomes the main desired product, while ironically social isolation goes dramatically up. By understanding how Japanese society has changed, one can learn much about the development of the West, too, which ultimately does affect problems such as antisemitism. One certainly cannot expect rates of Jew-hate to go down in societies with higher and higher numbers of people who are lonely, suffering from mental illness, and living in a virtual fantasy world. In this regard, Japan seems to the West to be several measurable clicks down the line when it comes to increased levels of loneliness fuelling a lacking capacity to critically understand the world and, as a result, more widespread stereotypes about Jews.

The Japanese, like Westerners, now have more opportunities for self-expression, but this is accompanied by fewer community experiences and less financial security. But interacting and cooperating within a group has been an essential part of human evolutionary success. Interestingly, behavioural scientist Clay

Routledge argues that the global surge in suicides can be attributed to a 'crisis of meaninglessness'.[83] And studies demonstrate that the more people feel a sense of belonging, the more they perceive life as meaningful.[84] These results are repeated in studies showing that people who feel lonely view life as less meaningful compared to those who feel strongly connected to other humans.[85] Perhaps unsurprisingly, one finds a rapid rise in xenophobia[86] and suicides in Japan. During the 2020 school year, Japan recorded 415 suicides among schoolchildren between the ages of six and eighteen alone.[87] The degree of loneliness and isolation can also be seen in the sad phenomenon of *kodokushi*, the 'lonely death' of elderly people who are found dead in their apartments after several days. Even simple human interactions, such as speaking to one's neighbours, can be uncommon in Japanese cities, as one 'hello' would bind one with the obligation to continue to greet that neighbour every time you see them, forever.

Lonely Japanese people may turn to hiring a 'husband', 'grandson', 'mother', or 'friend' with whom to spend time from agencies that run a thriving business renting out replacement relatives. One could argue that while the West is rather ethically oriented with its Judeo-Christian heritage, Japanese culture— with its Zen, Shinto, and Shingon Buddhism—is more aesthetically oriented. This is, of course, not to say that one is better than the other, and more a question of guilt versus shame. Going shopping with a rental grandchild may, therefore, seem more reasonable in an aesthetically oriented culture. Some overweight or single parents who are having trouble getting their child into a competitive school may, for example, hire a spouse or a slimmer parent for the interview if they feel this would make a better impression on the educators in a culture so focused on how aesthetically pleasing things are. In this culture, people might also take Instagram pictures with hired friends, so others are not ashamed of their loneliness. These cases are not mainstream in Japan, but they do seem to be increasing,[88] and they provide an insight into the common mentality in Japan of prioritizing aesthetic pleasure and the symbolic function, or representation, of people that is different from Western practices.

Other agencies offer women the opportunity to meet 'handsome men weeping', so clients can choose a 'tough guy', 'little brother', 'mixed race', or 'dentist' type of man who helps them cry. Other agencies, which currently number around forty in Japan, seek to achieve this by showing their clients sad videos in an atmosphere where they can feel comfortable crying.[89] The Japanese call this communal crying *rui-katsu*, a practice which is used to boost team spirit at companies, or to help provide earthquake survivors or mothers who lost their children with catharsis. This idea is not as alien to the West as one might think. Judaism and Christianity are familiar with the phenomenon of hired mourners (Amos 5:16; 2 Chronicles 35:25; Jeremiah 9:17–18), and Western societies believe in the transformation of strangers into loved ones: therapists, babysitters, nurses, and so on. But it speaks to an increasing culture of loneliness in Japan, where people fulfil a societal and symbolic role which is quite different from the Western emphasis on individualism. Therefore, this chapter is not only about Japanese–Jewish relations, but the Japanese 'Jewish' fantasy, or symbolic construction, which—just like the 'handsome dentist' crying with his clients, or the grandchild actor—is an aesthetic construction that has a symbolic function in the imagination of many Japanese people.

AN IMAGINED JEWISH-JAPANESE CONNECTION

To understand fantasies about Jews in Japan, one needs to understand the identity of those who produce and consume them. Many Japanese have certainly consumed misinformation about Jews through foreign sources, such as *The Protocols of the Elders of Zion*. Yet people in Japan have also been extraordinarily skilled at inventing their own extravagant fantasies about the Jews. Between 1877 and 1988 alone, they produced more than 5,500 books on the 'Jews'.[90] Not all of these are antisemitic, but many are, rather, about an imagined Jewish–Japanese connection, written with the intention of helping the Japanese understand their position in this world.

Several attempts have been made to shape theories that trace the Japanese people (or their emperor) to a lost tribe of Israel.[91]

In 1879, the Scotsman Norman McLeod published in Nagasaki a book in English he called *Japan and the Lost Tribes of Israel*. After 'personal research and observation', McLeod, who started his career in the herring industry before ending up in Korea and Japan as a missionary,[92] was surprised to see in Japan 'many Jewish faces similar to those I saw on the continent ... the emperor ... much resembles the noble Jewish family of Epstein ... and young [Princess] Fushimi no Miya has the most Israelitish countenance of any member of the Imperial Family'.[93] The book then goes on to argue that Shinto shrines resemble the two Temples in Jerusalem, due to being shaped like a tent or tabernacle, and because they are built of cedar.[94]

In 1908, another attempt was made to link both peoples, this time by a Japanese Christian, Saeki Yoshiro, who was professor at Waseda University.[95] He argued that the Uzumasa Shrine in Kyoto enshrines King David. His theory can be seen as the beginning of *Nichi-Yu dosoron*, the theory of the common ancestry of the Japanese and Jews. The same year Saeki Yoshiro published his ideas, the Shanghai Jewish weekly magazine, *Israel's Messenger*, published a ludicrous article entitled 'Japanese Jews', which argued that the *burakumin*—outcasts in Japan—were descendants of Jews.[96] Similar to the Jews of Europe, the *burakumin* were discriminated against in Japan and lived in their own communities, hamlets, or neighbourhoods. What the article wrongly imagined was that they resembled the 'Semitic type' rather than the Japanese, and that 'in the ghetto of Nagasaki, for instance, the Ety [*burakumin*] observe the Sabbath very religiously. Not only do they not work on that day of the week, but they do not smoke or kindle fires, just like the Orthodox Jew'.'[97]

In 1921, the same Jewish magazine published a letter by Elizabeth A. Gordon, former lady-in-waiting to Queen Victoria, claiming that 'many Hebrew words are said to exist in the dialects spoken around Kyoto'.[98] Those ideas, inspired by European Christian Zionism, influenced some Japanese and, in return, Jewish thinkers in the West. In 1942, the New York publication of the *Universal Jewish Encyclopedia* wrote:

A theory has been advanced that the Japanese are descendants of the Lost Ten Tribes of Israel ... Occidental travellers have found in the Yamato District of Japan two villages named Goshen and Menashe ... In the vicinity of the two villages there is still a temple known as David's Shrine.[99]

While contemporary scholars of Jewish studies deny these claims, such fantasies are still alive in Japan.[100] Juji Nakada, the first bishop of the Japan Holiness Church and co-founder of the Oriental Missionary Society (now One Mission Society), believed that the Japanese were the descendants of the ten lost tribes of Israel, and saw the Jews 'as mystical saviours whose redemption would ensure the political and military, as well as spiritual, salvation of the Japanese'.[101] He also preached that the Hebrew Bible was full of references to Japan, such as Ezekiel 43:2 ('And behold, the glory of the God of Israel was coming from the east.') or Isaiah 41:2 ('Tell me, who raised up that one from the east, one greeted by victory wherever he goes?').[102] Nowadays, the Holy Ecclesia of Jesus continues Nakada's spirit by maintaining hostels in Kyoto and other cities around Japan called 'Beit Shalom', in which Israelis can stay free of charge for up to three days, and by performing Hebrew songs on Israel's Independence Day.

Journalist Oya Soichi (after whom the Oya Soichi Nonfiction Award is named), published in 1959 the book *Nihon no jimbutsu komyaku* (The Human Veins of Ore of Japan), in which he claimed that the inhabitants of Shiga Prefecture (near Kyoto) are descendants of Jews because he considered them to have crooked noses. Kita Morio, a prominent novelist and psychiatrist, believed the Jewish people to be identical with the *tengu*, long-nosed mythical creatures in Japan.[103] In his 1961 bestseller *Dokutoru Mambo konchu-ki* (The Entomological Account of Doctor Mambo), he also argued the Ainu (indigenous people of northern Japan) might be of Jewish heritage due to their similar customs, such as the washing of hands before meals. In 1990, the *Isuraeru Jubozoku Kenkyu-kai* (Research Society for the Ten Tribes of Israel) was founded as a response to this rather odd argumentation.

The theory of the Japanese being a lost tribe of Israel certainly plays into a yearning felt by some Jews to be naturally a larger

47

group, as well as a desire felt by many Japanese to have deeper cultural roots that are not Chinese. Miyazawa Masanori has argued that the fantasy of the Japanese being a lost tribe of Israel serves as an attractive psychological defense against the West for some Japanese Christians.[104] It gives them an opportunity to solve the dilemma of being attracted to Christian morals but feeling threatened by Western culture by constructing an identity as the 'original Christians'.[105] In my experience of Japanese people in general, many tend to view Judaism as a Christian sect, which is not automatically the result of ignorance or lack of interest in foreign religions. Seen from a Japanese standpoint, Judaism and Christianity worship the same God, and both are based on the Old Testament as their religious text. One could argue that this view is perfectly reasonable, given that the difference between some Buddhist sects in Japan—for example, Zen and Shingon—is far greater than that between Judaism and Christianity.

While being popular all over the world, in no country other than the United States does Anne Frank's *Diary of a Young Girl* sell as well as it does in Japan.[106] As a result, Japan's first company to sell sanitary pads called itself 'Anne Co., Ltd', selling its products under the name *Anne no hi*—Anne's Day—which became a euphemism for menstruation in Japan.[107] However, the symbolic identification of many people in Japan with Anne Frank goes further by helping the Japanese redefine themselves as victims of the Second World War. Most people in Japan do not read the diary as the story of a Jewish Holocaust victim but, rather, in an *otaku* spirit as 'the prototype of all youth—helpless, imprisoned, at the mercy of elders, defiant of the outside world and terrified within'.[108] Similar to the reading of *The Diary of a Young Girl* in other countries, in Japan Anne Frank became a symbol of an isolated and threatened innocence. The symbolic function served by Anne Frank enabled people in Japan to relate to the victims of the Second World War and the Holocaust without feeling guilty about their contribution to it. In this regard, many Japanese also construct the bombing of Hiroshima and Nagasaki in relation to the Jewish experience in Europe during the Second World War by speaking of both equally as a 'holocaust'.

48

Many Japanese began to identify themselves with the Jewish people in order to establish themselves as innocent victims in the immediate aftermath of the Second World War. Osamu Dazei, considered one of the foremost fiction writers of twentieth-century Japan, wrote in his 1947 novel *Shayō* (The Setting Sun) of a family in decline in the post-war period of transition between a traditional and a more advanced Japanese society: 'I wonder if we are to blame, after all. Is it our fault that we were born aristocrats? Merely because we were born in such a family, we are condemned to spend our whole lives in humiliation, apologies, and abasement, like so many Jews.'[109]

Similarly, Fujita Den, founder of McDonald's in Japan and a board member of Softbank, identified himself after a commercial district in Tokyo in which he worked as a 'Ginza Jew':

> I am proud of being Japanese, but as a businessman I am happy being known as a Jew. Now Jews from around the world call me a 'Ginza Jew', too, and treat me like an insider. They treat me differently than gentiles. The title of 'Ginza Jew' is invaluable to me in doing business with Jewish traders who control business life in many countries. Nonetheless, there is no shortage of examples of how I was laughed at, stepped on and insulted by Jews. But I endured their insults just like the Jews have endured all their hardship.[110]

In his successful book, *The Jewish Way of Doing Business*, Fujita cited antisemitism as the reason behind the perceived discrimination he faced because of his Kansai dialect, and argued that Jews had settled in Osaka some thousand years before. This cultural appropriation and misrepresentation of Judaism as some kind of synonym for success is, of course, not solely a Japanese or East Asian phenomenon. Take, for example, the commerical activities of 'Kabbalah centres' across the West, or Caryn Elaine Johnson, the daughter of a Baptist clergyman with no Jewish background,[111] who decided to call herself 'Whoopi Goldberg' when she became an actress (and who on two later occasions defended Mel Gibson following recordings of his antisemitic rants being posted online[112] and said the Holocaust 'isn't about race').[113]

THE JAPANESE TALMUD

Masao Yamaguchi, a key figure in the introduction of anthropology to Japan, stated that he felt like the 'Jew among the Japanese'.[114] And the highly acclaimed Japanese novelist Shimada Masahiko, whom *The New York Times* called 'proof that the Japanese novel is taking some fantastic turns in the hands of a new generation of writers',[115] explored the idea of becoming a Jew in 'A Callow Fellow of Jewish Descent'.[116] It would, however, be wrong to assume that these writers have spent much time studying Judaism itself and discovering it beyond any symbolic function, before making their claims. Kita Morio, for example, believes that 'Judaism is a religion that worships the sun'.[117] But, as Norman Cohn put it so well in *Warrant for Genocide*: 'It is a great mistake to suppose that the only writers who matter are those whom the educated in their saner moments can take seriously.'[118]

What currently shapes the image of the Jewish people in Japan the most is the Talmud or, rather, an idea of it. Books (supposedly) dealing with the Talmud, are in fact bestsellers in Japan. The Talmud, or what people believe it to be, was first made popular in Japan by Marvin Tokayer (see Chapter 1). As in South Korea, someone looking for a copy of the Talmud in Japan will eventually come across Rabbi Tokayer's books, such as *Five Thousand Years of Jewish Wisdom: Secrets of the Talmud Scriptures*. Many even contain a picture of him inside their front covers. One only needs to browse through some of the Tokayer publications—for example, *There Is No Education in Japan: The Jewish Secret of Educating Geniuses*—to see how unethical they are. While searching 'Talmud' on Amazon. co.jp, hundreds of Japanese-language titles appear, like *The Habit of Getting Big Money and Success From a Single Sentence Sent to a Grandchild by a 99-Year-Old Jewish Super Businessman*, or *Recipe for Jewish Genius Education*. This commercialization of the Talmud and Judaism by Tokayer and authors that followed him has further inflamed myths in Japan of the Jews being different from other people.

POLITICAL IMPLICATIONS

There have been implications of philo- and antisemitism in the political realm. There exists a Japan Kibbutz Association (*Nihon

Kibutsu Kyokai), which at its height contained 30,000 members.[119] In 1965, one of its members, Ishihama Mikaru, published the bestseller *Shalom Israel*, in which she described the friendliness she had encountered in Israel. Another repercussion of philosemitism in Japan is the Christian Zionist Makuya movement which, with over 300,000 Japanese subscribers to their newsletter, seems to be growing fast. Verifying membership numbers has proved difficult, however, since the movement seeks not to give an exact number in a reference to David's sinful census of his fighting men in 2 Samuel 24:2. Makuya (Tabernacle) honours Judaism for its gifts to Christianity, uses the menorah as its symbol instead of the cross, and occasionally holds pro-Israel demonstrations in Tokyo. Every member of the movement receives a Hebrew name after completing a pilgrimage to Israel, where one might encounter them joyfully singing Hebrew songs in the streets of Jerusalem. But there has also been the Lod Airport Massacre of 30 May 1972, in which three Japanese terrorists attacked Lod Airport (now Ben Gurion International Airport) murdering twenty-six people, including the renowned protein biophysicist and candidate for the upcoming Israeli presidency election, Professor Aharon Katzir, and injuring eighty others.[120]

While the political left in Japan has tended to be critical of Israel since the Six-Day War, the political right is rather sympathetic to it. Admiration for the State of Israel has become a part of Japanese philosemitism in sections of the political right, which seems to admire the Jewish State for what they perceive as its influence on the United States.

In general, Japanese anti- and philosemitism spring from the country's strong feelings of insecurity in the modern world. The level to which the Japanese public tends to mistrust the media and political institutions is increasing. In 2019, Genron, a Japanese think tank, found that 60 per cent of the people surveyed did not trust political parties and did 'not expect them to solve issues'.[121] Japan's modern existential crisis contributes to an extreme political culture where people are not as much divided by different ideologies as they are united in a search for meaning wherever they can find it. While antisemitism and philosemitism in the West are morally driven, attributing bad or good qualities to the Jewish people, 'the Jew' serves a symbolic function in Japan and follows a different, non-Western, cultural logic. In response to the process of globalization, this has gone as far as fetishizing the Jewish people as being geniuses and business prodigies. Studying their way of being and dealing with them as symbols has become a modern fantasy amongst many Japanese, almost a sort of magic for finding personal fortune. Other times it has led to forms of antisemitism where Jews serve as symbols of something evil without even being present in the country. Tellingly, when a Japanese mission went to Germany to study the Nazi movement in 1932, a member of the mission was asked what he thought of the movement. He replied: 'It is magnificent. I wish we could have something like it in Japan, only we can't, because we haven't got any Jews.'[122]

JEWISH-JAPANESE HISTORY

Japan would do well by emphasizing its own, factual, Jewish history: the European Jews who were forced to convert to Christianity and then fled to Nagasaki, where they were able to revert to Judaism in 1572. Or Chiune Sugihara, the 'Japanese Oskar Schindler', who, as vice-consul in Lithuania helped thousands of Jews flee the Nazis by issuing them transit visas, and whom Yad Vashem has recognized as a 'Righteous Among the Nations'. To this day, little effort has been made to publicize his actions to the Japanese public.[123] Nor, to my knowledge, do the Japanese learn in school or from the media about the American soldiers of Japanese descent who liberated the Dachau concentration camp.[124] Wolf Isaac Ladejinsky, the 'father' of Japan's highly successful land reform in the late 1940s and early 1950s, is not known by most Japanese, either. Similarly obscure in Japan is the name of Beate Sirota Gordon, the 22-year-old American Jewish woman who wrote Article 14, Paragraph 1 of the post-Second World War Japanese Constitution: 'All of the people are equal under the law and there shall be no discrimination in political, economic or social relations because of race, creed, sex, social status or family origin.'[125]

3

TAIWANESE JAIL

One could describe it as an admiration beyond political tactics. Chiang Kai-shek was leader of the Kuomintang political party and the Republic of China, and later founder of the 'Republic of China, Taiwan', which he ruled as a dictator from 1950 until his death in 1975. His personality cult in Taiwan remains very much alive, as evinced by several statues of the former dictator still standing, and the fact that most of the population knows by heart a memorial song written after his death, as they have to memorize it in school. Moreover, the National Chiang Kai-shek Memorial Hall was constructed after his death, covering over 240,000 square metres in central Taipei, and remains one of the country's landmarks. The New York Public Library Digital Collection allows anyone to read the English translation of an admiring letter Chiang Kai-shek sent to Hitler on 16 September 1936:

> Your Excellency! Herr Reichskanzler I give you my most sincere thanks for sending General von Reichenau to me as your special emissary. The choice of his personality was a special honor for me ... The thoughts of Your Excellency ... are a special joy to me ... You, Herr Reichskanzler ... had the honorary sword of the German Reich given to me. I take it as a symbol of soldierly loyalty and as a true sign of the friendly relationship of our countries. With my best wishes for your personal health and the

well being of your country I am Your Excellency's loyal (signed) Marshall Chiang Kai Shek.[1]

Von Reichenau was a war criminal who issued the Severity Order which encouraged German soldiers to murder Jewish civilians on the Eastern Front. Wang Jingwei, a member of the Kuomintang, visited Nazi Germany in 1936, reporting back that 'Several advanced countries have already expanded their national vitality and augmented their people's strength, and are no longer afraid of foreign aggression'.[2] Kuomintang official H.H. Kung, along with two other officials, visited Germany in 1937 and was received by Hitler. And Alexander von Falkenhausen, who later during the German occupation of Belgium became head of its military government from 1940–4 and who was responsible for the murder and deportation of Jews,[3] was a military advisor to Chiang Kai-shek.[4]

Chiang Kai-shek's nationalists were responsible for the deaths of millions of innocent people in mainland China.[5] The Kuomintang under Chiang Kai-shek cooperated with the Nazis until the Second Sino-Japanese War in 1937, when Germany decided to back Japan. At the November 1947 General Assembly vote on the partition of Palestine into a Jewish state and an Arab state, Chiang Kai-shek (while head of the Republic of China, then in mainland China) abstained. This was a shift from earlier Chinese support for Zionism. In 1920, Dr Sun Yat-sen, known as the father of modern China, called Zionism 'one of the greatest movements of the present time', and he wrote to a Zionist author in Shanghai, 'All lovers of Democracy cannot help but support whole-heartedly and welcome with enthusiasm the movement to restore your wonderful and historic nation.'[6]

In Taipei, a Holocaust-themed restaurant, called 'Jail', was described as 'pushing the boundaries of taste as it invites diners to chow down under the gaze of Nazi concentration camp victims'. Its décor included photographs of Auschwitz victims on the walls and open pipes and valves in the toilets, which were called 'gas chambers'.[7] (When I presented these findings at a conference in Jerusalem, a 'Jewish and Israel studies' scholar from mainland

China responded with the disturbing comment that restaurant guests were just 'expressing their admiration of Jewish culture'.) Another restaurant in NewTaipei City had a dish on the menu called 'Long Live the Nazis'. After Israeli and German representatives in Taiwan complained, the restaurant changed the name of the dish to 'Long Live Purity'.[8] What's more, one can easily find businesses in Taiwan that use Nazi symbols to market everything from sports shoes to cars to German-made electric heaters, whose mascot is a cartoon Hitler. In 2011, for instance, supermarkets in Taiwan sold keychains featuring a cartoon version of a vampire Hitler.[9]

In 2001, Taiwan's Democratic Progressive Party (DPP)—the leading Congressional party at the time, and, at the time of writing, ruling Congress and the President's office withTsai Ing-wen—ran a TV commercial using images of Hitler to encourage Taiwan's youth to engage in politics and speak their own minds.[10] The head of Israel's representation in Taiwan, Menashe Zipori, called the election advertisement 'an insult to humanity', and stated that even had the Taiwanese party used Hitler 'out of pure ignorance or a lack of awareness', this would not be an excuse.[11] And, indeed, a DPP spokesman stated in response to the critique, 'we fully understand the history of the Jews'.[12] After the incident, the Israeli newspaper *Haaretz* reported that 'a number of supporters of the Taiwanese party [DPP] had called the Israeli office and had threatened to protest the Israeli reaction to the advertisement. Taiwanese foreign ministry subsequently ordered that security around the office be beefed up'.[13]

The country is the home of the so-called 'National Socialism Association in Taiwan', an NGO under Taiwanese law that champions Hitler and blames democracy for Taiwan's 'social unrest'[14] (whatever that might mean in such a tightly organised country as Taiwan).

Paul Lin's essay in the *Taipei Times*, 'Israel, Jews and US-China relations',[15] is another example of antisemitism in Taiwan. International media like *The Algemeiner* also reported an incident at the Hsinchu Kuang Fu High School in Hsinchu City where 'students [were] wearing SS uniforms, and waving Nazi flags while they march, as their history teacher portrays Adolf Hitler. One photo captures a student riding a cardboard "tank" and performing the Nazi salute'.[16] A statement by Asher Yarden, an envoy at the Israeli Economic and Cultural Office in Taipei, declared in response:

> It is deplorable and shocking that seven decades only after the world had witnessed the horrors of the Holocaust, a high school in Taiwan is supporting such an outrageous action as we witnessed yesterday at Hsinchu Kuang Fu Senior High School. We strongly condemn this tasteless occurrence and call on the Taiwanese authorities, at all levels, to initiate educational programs which would introduce the meaning of the Holocaust and teach its history and universal meaning. Israel would support such endeavors as may be necessary.[17]

And Israel's former representative to Taiwan, Raphael Gamzou, spoke of there being a 'psychological and social sickness' with a 'nostalgia for monsters as role model[s]' in Taiwan.[18] Articles such as 'Sad old anti-Semitic stereotypes' by Ross Feingold, chairman of the Taipei Jewish Center, give further indication of the prevalence of antisemitism in the country.[19] The Simon Wiesenthal Center and the ADL both published press releases decrying the events, but which suddenly became unavailable to access online (as of 30 March 2023).[20]

In a small country, only about twice the size of Hawaii, those incidents do count, and especially given Taiwan's human rights record, with violations ranging from possible death penalties levied for the use of illegal drugs to the forced hospitalization of mentally and socially challenged persons.[21] And being homeless, fighting too much in public, or laughing too loudly on the subway are all behaviours which might be seen as 'insane' and result in someone being forced into hospitalization. I have witnessed this myself when a peaceful homeless man near the campus of National Chengchi University was suddenly arrested and disappeared for good.

Media outlets such as the BBC have also reported on racism in Taiwan, especially towards Westerners dating local women.[22] Visitors to Taiwan might fall victim to the general culture of mistrust against foreigners, who often get accused by locals of having committed all kinds of crimes and as a result are prevented by the authorities from leaving the island. This can have dramatic consequences for anyone who does not speak Chinese, especially in a system where people have to prove their innocence rather than the onus being on the authorities to prove their guilt.[23]

The few scholars who address antisemitism in Taiwan have, unfortunately, largely minimized or denied the problem: for example, Meron Medzini, who also denies in his work the Nanjing Genocide,[24] claimed that 'There have been no reports of anti-Semitism' in the country;[25] and Mor Sobol, who writes most positively about the Taiwanese government in *Israel Affairs*.[26] In his work, Sobol finds incidents of antisemitism in Taiwan to be 'more the result of ignorance (and lack of sensitivity) than anti-Semitism', since this was how it had been explained to him by Taiwanese officials.[27] This is, of course, problematic, and both Israeli officials and the Jewish community in Taiwan have raised their concern.

Another of Sobol's contributions to *Israel Affairs* attempts to explain why Taiwan is free of antisemitism: President Tsai visited Israel before taking office and published an article in a Taiwanese newspaper 'that conveyed her admiration for Israel's security, technological, and economic capabilities'.[28] Following this line of arguing, one would have to view other political figures—such as Nixon, who visited Israel and admired it for its technology and economy—in a more generous light as well.[29] When faced with criticism for Sobol's article,[30] *Israel Affairs* then published a 'correspondence' by a self-identified 'rightist-conservative' political activist who wants to 'restore the sacred Chinese nation'.[31] One should put 'Beijing on trial' goes the argument of the 'correspondence' in defence of Taiwan, as if Taiwan can be automatically excused from all criticism by comparing it to mainland China, or, rather, must be excused for political reasons, even if all facts point to the contrary.[32]

Even while Jonathan Goldstein dedicated his book *Jewish Identities in East and Southeast Asia* to Taiwan's Jewish community, he thanked a group of people for their 'research assistance'[33] some of whose backgrounds and previous work on the topic are surprising, to say the least.[34] His views on the issue of antisemitism differ greatly from mine, such as when he writes about the 'nurturing conditions'[35] Jews would live under in Taiwan's 'Oasis of Tranquillity',[36] and about there being 'no history of anti-Semitism on the island and no state religion'.[37] Nor is his argument about the lack of a state religion one I find particularly convincing. Taiwan doesn't officially have a state religion. Nor does Syria.[38] But Norway does have one, and so do Iceland, England, and Malta. However, if one defines 'state religion' as less official, as a religion influencing the state, one could argue that Confucianism, which does influence Taiwan, to be a state religion. Goldstein also claims that 'Incidents of anti-Semitism in Taiwan are rare and seem to have been inadvertent'.[39] But if antisemitism were 'inadvertent', one would call it a misunderstanding, not antisemitism.

But it isn't. Fact is, Taiwan does struggle with antisemitism, and very much so. This is combined with instances of a fetishized admiration of an imagined Jewish success in business that derives from Japanese 'Talmud' publications. One could, for instance, book a room in the 'Talmud Business Hotel' in central Taichung, whose website describes it as:

> Talmud Hotel—GongYuan is a Business hotel that is named after a holy book contain[ing] a collection of ancient rabbinic writings on Jewish law and traditions. The word Talmud has the following meanings: 'Instruction, Learning, Teach and Study'. Inspired by the Talmud theory, the owner uses red interior to add a splash of fashion and professionalism. In each room, there's also a copy of 'Talmud-Business Success Bible' for anyone who would like to experience the Talmud way of becoming successful.[40]

But for anyone who instead would like to experience an understanding of the Jewish people that is free of antisemitism, a realistic worldview awaits. This is something Taiwan, which is still struggling with its international recognition and dictatorial past, could certainly do well with.

4

HISTORICAL MEMORY IN HONG KONG

Since 2002, Erica Lyons has called Hong Kong home. According to her website, she is not only a TEDx speaker; the founder/editor-in-chief of *Asian Jewish Life—A Journal of Spirit, Society and Culture*, a magazine celebrating the 'diversity of the Jewish experience in Asia'; and the Hong Kong delegate to the World Jewish Congress, but also Chairwoman of the Jewish Historical Society of Hong Kong. Unfortunately, there currently is not a single Jewish studies programme at any of the city's top eleven institutions of higher education, which puts the Society and Lyons in a more important position. In an interview with *The Jewish Chronicle*, Lyons stated that during the Japanese occupation of Hong Kong during the Second World War,

> many Jews were interned in prisoner of war camps but that it had nothing to do with being Jewish or not Jewish. They weren't treated any differently [to others] in the camps. I think that the Japanese didn't really understand antisemitism. Certainly, people suffered terribly during the war, but Jews were never a target, more than any other ally. And in fact Jews in Hong Kong—and not just during that time—we have never suffered from antisemitism at all.[1]

Similarly, Glen Steinman, Co-Chairman of the Hong Kong Holocaust and Tolerance Centre, has stated: 'Antisemitism is a disease and it can be contagious. So we want to make sure that the contagion doesn't spread here.'[2] Steinman doesn't see any root for antisemitism in Hong Kong, whose people 'tend to have a "fascination"' with Jewish culture rather than prejudice towards it. There's a sympathy but there's also a desire to know more'.[3] These observations seemingly ignore occasional incidents of Islamic antisemitism in Hong Kong, which is home to an estimated 300,000 Muslims (of whom about 150,000 are Indonesian, 50,000 are Chinese, and 30,000 are Pakistani),[4] as well as the many publications on 'Jewish business' or 'Jewish wisdom and success' one can buy in bookshops across town. It is also worth mentioning that during the Second World War the Japanese forced the Jewish refugees under their occupation into a ghetto in Shanghai, where about 10 per cent of them died due to the miserable living conditions while the Japanese authorities continued to step up restrictions.[5] Moreover, under Japanese rule the Jews of Penang (in current-day Malaysia) were forced to wear the Star of David with the word 'Jew' written on it.[6] If they 'did not understand antisemitism', as Lyons put it, they certainly knew how to exercise it.

There is also a rather disturbing fetishization in Hong Kong not directly of Jews, but of the Holocaust. During the protests in Hong Kong that started in 2019, Holocaust images were omnipresent throughout the city (and Twitter), such as pictures of the inside of Nazi concentration camps and swastikas. Of course, this should not be confused with the swastika as a religious symbol in Asia, which is prevalent in Buddhist monasteries, temples, and communities, and on textiles, buildings, texts, and decorative objects. Other non-Buddhist religions in Hong Kong, such as Guiyidao, also use swastikas. The Guiyidao philanthropic branch, the 'Red Swastika Society', runs two schools in Hong Kong. However, in its religious meaning the swastika is not a symbol that people use during protests, and those seen at the Hong Kong protests should be understood as Nazi symbols, especially in the context of the frequent fetishization of Nazi iconography in East Asia. Simon K. Li of the Hong Kong Holocaust and Tolerance Center shows this in his research on Nazi-chic weddings, Nazi cosplay, or Nazi scandals in K-pop.[7]

The term 'Chinazi', a portmanteau of 'China' and 'Nazi', was frequently used by many protesters in such slogans as 'anti-Chinazi' or 'Stop Chinazi!', with pictures displayed of Hong Kong's Chief Executive Carrie Lam as Hitler. On 29 September 2019, the eightieth anniversary of Germany invading Poland, protesters in Hong Kong planned a 'Global Anti-ChiNazi March'.[8] A comparison between China and the Nazis predates the 2019 Hong Kong protests. I was able to trace it back to at least the 2018 book *Nazi China* by exiled Chinese author Yu Jie. Chinese state media has also fallen into the same tragic mistake, describing protesters themselves as 'Blacknazi'.[9] By using these images and words, the protesters intended to compare how they viewed Chinese Communist rule with Nazism. However, by using images of Jewish suffering in order to get the world's attention, not only do they trivialize the Holocaust but they also miss an opportunity to tell their own story to the world. Moreover, it is surprising that protesters, as well as the Chinese government, are not using references for evil that are closer to their own history, such as the Japanese occupation, but are rather fixating on words and symbols connected to the Holocaust and Jewish suffering.

5

'JEWS' BY AND FOR THE CHINESE

Most of Chinese-Jewish history took place in three cities: Kaifeng in central China, with its Jewish community tracing back to the Middle Ages; the northern city of Harbin, which, especially after the Bolshevik revolution in Russia, hosted a Jewish expat community; and Shanghai, where the Yangtze River meets the Pacific Ocean and much of China's contact to the rest of world unfolds. Shanghai's Jewish community has been established since the nineteenth century, which saw Sephardi Jews immigrating from India, Iraq, and Egypt.[1] During the Holocaust, China became a haven for Jews from Europe thanks to the help of people like Ho Feng-Shan, who served as Chinese consul-general in Vienna and saved thousands of Jews from the Nazis by issuing them visas. (In 2000, the Israeli organization Yad Vashem recognized him as a 'Righteous Among the Nations'.) Yet, during the Japanese occupation of Shanghai, Jews suffered as the Japanese forced Jewish refugees—at first about 20,000 of them, and later all Jews but the Russians—to live in an area of approximately one square mile in the Hongkew district, and increasingly stepped up restrictions after that.[2] The area was a slum with about twice the population density of present-day Manhattan, where ten people lived in a single room and with near starvation, disastrous sanitation, scant employment, rampant disease, and isolation.[3] Two thousand of the

Shanghai Ghetto's (formally known as the Restricted Sector for
Stateless Refugees) Jewish inhabitants—roughly 10 per cent—
died during the few years of the Ghetto's existence, due to the
miserable living conditions created by the Japanese occupiers.
Xiao Xian, scholar at Yunnan University, wrote of the Chinese
people's knowledge of Jews that

> Although Jews lived in China for centuries, the Chinese people
> were long unaware that these people were part of a worldwide
> Diaspora. Not until the European powers forced open China's
> closed door in the second half of the nineteenth century did the
> Chinese begin to know about Jews in the outside world and to
> connect them with the small Jewish community inside China.[4]

Jews remained largely a minority, and if noticed at all they were called
by various different names, one being Yi-ci-le-ye (Chosen People).[5]
Nowadays, the Jews of China officially do not exist as a legal group
but are seen merely as 'descendents'.[6] They are not among the fifty-
six recognized minorities in China,[7] while there are reports of them
being under state pressure as a group.[8] Judaism is also not one of
the officially recognized religions in the People's Republic of China
unlike Buddhism, Daoism, Islam, Catholicism, and Protestantism.

JEWS IN THE CHINESE POPULAR IMAGINATION

With Jews being an extremely small minority in the country (they
currently number about 2,500[9] out of 1.4 billion, or 0.00018
per cent), most people from mainland China have never met a
Jew. However, Gilya Gerda Schmidt describes Chinese interest in
Judaism and the State of Israel as 'widespread and genuine'.[10] And
this interest has not gone unnoticed among scholars who otherwise
tend to neglect the rest of East Asia in that regard. Irene Eber writes
about the history of Jews in China and translations of Chinese
literature into Hebrew.[11] Galia Patt-Shamir and Yaov Rapoport
talk about the similarities between Judaism and Confucianism.[12]
But when they claim that 'the Chinese are completely innocent
of anti-Semitism',[13] they are certainly mistaken, especially if
we look at antisemitism in Chinese cyberspace.[14] In his book

Shanghai Sanctuary, Bei Gao ended a widespread misconception of Japan acting in any way 'pro-Jewish' during the occupation of China during the Second World War.[15] Glenn Timmermans points to the lack of Holocaust studies programmes at universities in China,[16] while Salomon Wald reports on a vast majority of Chinese students being familiar with the Holocaust as a historical fact and their tendency to compare it to Chinese suffering under Japanese occupation during the Second World War.[17] Chinese scholar Zhou Xun interestingly writes about the place Jews take in Chinese imagination, which she finds complex. According to her, in the Chinese imagination, "Jew" is

> a symbol for money, deviousness, and meanness; it can also represent poverty, trustworthiness, and warm heartedness. It has religious and well as secular meanings. While it represents individualism, it also stands for a collective spirit. On the one hand, it is the symbol for tradition; on the other hand it can equally invoke modernity ... anything which is not Chinese is Jewish, at the same time anything which is Chinese is also Jewish; anything which the Chinese need is Jewish, at the same time anything which the Chinese despise is Jewish.[18]

James R. Ross writes about the image of Jews in popular Chinese culture, and he tells of many bestsellers in China that deal with how Jews allegedly make money and raise their children, which certainly are creating more stereotypes.[19] M. Avrum Ehrlich argues that when it comes to China, 'for the most part, the cultural and theological underpinnings of European anti-Semitism are not understood, have no appeal, and do not resonate within Chinese culture'.[20] However, he can't help but note that 'books have been published [in China] which in other countries would represent gross generalizations and distortions, and border on anti-Semitism'.[21] Mostly, it must be said these publications have already crossed the line into antisemitic and/or philosemitic content, as they fetishize a perceived Jewish form of success, such as: *Complete Book of Jewish Super Wisdom*, *Secrets of Jewish Millionaires*, *Strangers From Mars: Nobel Prize and Jew*, and some of the more outrageously antisemitic titles, such as *Jewish Conspiracy of Destroying the World*.[22]

Other titles translate as *The Eight Most Valuable Business Secrets of the Jewish*,[23] *Why Are the Jews Capable of Making Money? Unlocking the World's Foremost Merchants' Money-Making Secrets*,[24] *The Legend of Jewish Wealth*,[25] or *Jewish People and Business: The Bible of How to Live Their Lives*.[26] These books go back to the Japanese product of the 'Talmud', which becomes evident with books such as *Japanese and Jewish Secrets of Making Money*,[27] or *Talmud: Jewish Bible on Business and Living*.[28] Some estimate that sales of 'success books' make up nearly a third of books sold in mainland China, and 'perhaps no type of success book has been as well marketed or well received as those that purport to unveil the secrets of Jewish entrepreneurs. Many of these books sell upward of 30,000 copies a year'.[29] Quite similarly to books in Korean or Japanese, these publications have little to do with Judaism, but rather use the 'Talmud' and 'Judaism' to sell business-related self-help, with case studies on the Rothschilds, the Lehman brothers, or people who are mistakenly presented as Jewish like J.P. Morgan or John D. Rockefeller. Many of these books are written pseudonymously by fake authors with Western names like 'William Hampton' that to the Chinese ear perhaps sound somehow Jewish. He Xiong Fe, visiting professor at Nankai University's Literature Department, estimates that 'more than half of the books are fakes, written by people who are not familiar with Judaism or Jewish history and who have made up their qualifications',[30] while at the same time he himself has lectured on such topics as 'Why are Jewish people so smart?' and 'The mystery of the Jews'.[31]

Most Chinese have never had any clear idea of who exactly a Jew is. Unsurprisingly, books such as *Jews, a People of Mystery* (Xiao Xian, 2000) or *Israel—The Mysterious Country* (Yang Menzu, 1992) have appeared. Stereotypes about the Jewish people in mainland China are about their wealth, political power, and contributions to twentieth-century Western civilization, especially those of Einstein and Marx. '[A]dmiration is mixed with some envy, but not hostility,'[32] and such Jewish success stories are seen as a result of an emphasis on education across their culture. Sinologist Joseph Levenson found a 'paramount importance of historical thinking in Chinese culture',[33] which could explain why many Chinese intellectuals, contrary to the Jewish historical experience in Christian or Muslim societies,

> are attracted by the longevity and continuity of the Jewish people through three thousand or more years, and like to compare it to their own long history. In a display of traditional Chinese politeness, some affirm to Jewish visitors that the Jews have five thousand years of history and may thus claim even greater age than the Chinese. This can result in a feeling of affinity which few other nations share.[34]

Ariana Eunjung Cha wrote in the *Washington Post* on how Jewish businesspeople in China are 'bombarded with invitations to give seminars on how to make money "the Jewish way".' She further argues: 'The business success books provide idealized notions of what Chinese people should strive to become and serve as templates for teaching people who have been working at communist, state-owned enterprises for a generation how to transform themselves as capitalists.'[35] Tuvia Gering, a China expert at the Jerusalem Institute for Strategy and Security, tells on the other hand of what he calls the 'intellectual antisemites' in China. Especially shocking are the conclusions of the prominent professor Zhang Wenmu of Beihang University, who derives from his study of Marx and Lenin such unacceptable nonsense as that the Jews put Hitler into power, control US foreign policy, or are responsible for the Russia-Ukraine conflict.[36]

Elite Reference (a Chinese newsweekly with a distribution of about 400,000) published an article with the title 'Do the Jews really control the United States', which queries: 'The total number of Jews in the world doesn't reach twenty million people, with only six million in America. In American commerce, finance, oil, construction, media, film etc. [Jews] hold important positions. Some people sigh, "America controls the world, and the Jews control America." So, is this true after all?'[37] The article continues with Kissinger's influence on Nixon and Ford and how many of the richest Americans were supposedly Jewish. 'But that's where the piece takes a distinctly Chinese turn,' notes Evan Osnos, a staff writer for *The New Yorker*. '[T]he author answers his titular question with a hopeful yes, noting that the Jewish people—known to be "permeated with wisdom, full of wit and talent"—the people who gave us Einstein, Freud, Marx, Spielberg—occupy a healthy position of influence in America.'[38] But Ehrlich observes in this regard that

> In the European context, the relationship of government and citizenry to its Jewish population was often an indicator of general tolerance levels and openness of society. The Chinese, perhaps aware of this, are careful to ensure that any hatred for Jews is not expressed. It is conceivable that attempts to express anti-Semitic opinions are repressed and internet sites blocked. The near-complete absence of open anti-Semitic material is so abnormal it suggests interference and censorship in the free expression of thought. Perhaps this is a positive step, but it may also suggest the intentional desire to be presented as a society tolerant of others.[39]

Frank Dikötter traces antisemitism in China back to the beginning of the twentieth century and the construction of a Chinese 'race'.[40] While a sense of humiliation and inferiority was prevalent among the radicals of China's reformers, 'the Jews' often served as an example of an even more humiliated group, which the reformers used as a symbol to boost the morale of their fellow Chinese. Jews have also served as an example of how a people without a homeland are vulnerable to suffering greater dangers, which Chinese intellectuals frequently used during the Japanese invasion in the 1930s.[41] The fate of the Jews thus served to mobilise the Chinese, not to induce empathy.

The level at which scholars currently rank antisemitism in the People's Republic of China is relatively high. Some antisemitism derives from the Islamic radicalization of some members of Muslim minorities in China,[42] although these constitute a very small portion of the overall population. In its 2014 poll, the Anti-Defamation League detected a level of antisemitism in mainland China of 20 per cent, which was equivalent to that of Italy.[43] The phenomenon must be seen within the general and ongoing problem of racism in China, which Dikötter pointed out in his brilliant book *The Discourse of Race in Modern China*.

Interestingly, over several years of living in China, Ehrlich conducted a number of surveys, questionnaires, and interviews of primarily college students.[44] In conclusion, he observed that

> Only rarely is praise given freely, without the will to share the credit or to reference the praise towards themselves. The conclusions drawn from this observation include the possibility that praise for 'the Jews' reflects an image of what the respondents would like to be or what they think they are, with the symbol of the 'Jews' merely serving as an image of their hopes and ambitions.[45]

This resonated with Zhang Shui's observation that Jewish studies in China serves to demonstrate the superiority of Chinese culture and the Han race: 'In order to have a real deep understanding of the vitality of Chinese culture, one must first study the interesting anthropological fact that the Hebrew race, well known for immutability, was assimilated by the Han race and became Chinese-Jewish descendants after entering China.'[46] This, of course, is nothing unique to China, as Jews have always integrated in large numbers to all kinds of societies throughout history. Around the world, people with no knowledge of having any Jewish ancestor taking a DNA test and suddenly finding themselves to be of some percentage Jewish speaks to this. It is not just Chinese culture that has attracted Jews into giving up their identity and religion (or taking part in creating another identity); many cultures have done so. The profound way many Jews had come to identify with German culture and nationality prior to the rise of the Nazis is such an example. The Kaifeng Jewish community was simply too small to survive the natural human tendency to integrate into a larger society.

Ehrlich further describes something quite interesting when he tells of Chinese students of Jewish studies:

> At the start of my class I opened with a series of contrasts between Chinese and Jews; I described how different they were and how they reflect entirely antithetical social dynamics. Some of the students, who had been excited to learn about Jews and Judaism, were noticeably uncomfortable, and for a short period of time seemed less interested in the subject. The Chinese

conscientiously try to find similarities and harmony in their relationships and circumstances, and the notion of existing and cooperating with something irreconcilably different is new and somehow threatening.[47]

There are two stories one could get from this: either that Chinese people are rather antisemitic but do not show it openly due to the government's wish for the country to appear tolerant of others, so they mix their antisemitism with admiration, or that Chinese people generally do not have the feeling that they must make a decision on the matter. Even though they make decisions about all kinds of things at any moment in their lives, when it comes to Jews they are beset with uncertainty. Ultimately, this may result in Chinese people reproducing two extreme stories they were exposed to in the search for harmony, as Jews are only a story to them and of importance only in their symbolic function.

CHINESE JEWISH STUDIES

Unfortunately, Jewish studies scholarship in China does not help much to unravel this. It has not developed sufficiently for it to be called a fully scientific endeavour. Xu Xin, of the Guilford Glazer Centre for Jewish Studies in Nanjing, started teaching this subject back in 1984 without having ever met a single Jew.[48] In 1992, after China recognized the State of Israel, he established the first Institute of Jewish Studies in his country, because of 'a growing demand for Judaic Studies in China'.[49] Since then, several universities have established centres for Jewish studies, and an academic conversation has flourished, mainly between China and Jewish studies scholars in the United States.[50] Yet, this has not always led to the best exchanges.[51]

Ehrlich notes:

Even in Chinese academic circles, the impressions of Jews continue to be in step with broad and superficial generalizations about race, culture and religion, which is unacceptable in contemporary Western intellectual etiquette, as it is believed that these have sometimes formed the basis for anti-Semitic campaigns

70

in the West. In China they are believed to be, at worst, harmless musings about world cultures.'[52]

Fu Youde of Shandong University's Center for Judaic and Inter-Religious Studies, for example, published an essay titled 'Why the Jews Are Wise' about the 'anti-traditional spirit' and 'their [the Jews'] learning habits'.[53] And Zhou Guojian, deputy dean of the Center for Jewish Studies at the Shanghai Academy of Social Sciences, believes Jews to be some kind of cure for the 'Chinese restaurant syndrome', a term he uses to refer to the Chinese being 'content with small-scale enterprises; they are happy just to make a living. But Jewish people want to be the best and make a huge company'.[54] This would explain, according to him, the fascination with Jews in China.

The work of Song Lihong, deputy director of the Glazer Institute of Jewish and Israel Studies at Nanjing University, is another example worthy of scrutiny. He claims that Chinese bestsellers— such as *Unveiling the Secrets of Jewish Success in World Economy*, *Talmud: The Greatest Jewish Bible for Making Money*, or *Currency Wars* (a book of 'cult status' telling how the Rothschild family allegedly seeks to control the world economy)—do not generally 'betray a kind of Judeophobia because the religious underpinnings of anti-Semitism in Europe and in Arab lands was and is irrelevant in China'.[55] Unfortunately, he misses the point with this argument since antisemitism can also flourish in countries without these histories and religious backgrounds. 'I can't be an antisemite because I'm Chinese' sounds all too familiar to the 'I can't be an antisemite, I have Jewish co-workers/a Jewish friend!' defence. The best example refuting this argument is the way Song Lihong's own work seemingly reflects antisemitic tendencies when he argues that Jewish studies in China are able to flourish specifically because the field is free of Jewish scholars:

> The modern scientific study of Jews and Judaism, from its beginnings in the *Wissenschaft des Judentums* to the present, is by and large Jewishly bound and fraught ... What looms largest behind these tensions and dilemmas is the intertwined nexus between critical Jewish learning and Jewish faith. In contrast, Chinese

Jewish studies, produced—at least predominantly—by and for the Chinese, could be described as Jewish studies independent of Jewish faith and without an intent to cultivate and strengthen Jewish identity; hence Chinese Jewish studies is freed of the burden of searching for its role both in the academy and in the tradition of Jewish learning, a fate that even today's non-Jewish scholars of Jews and Judaism in Germany can hardly escape.[56]

'Jews' often fulfil contradictory symbolic functions for Chinese scholars, who connect them to a Western (mostly American) field of study while at the same time viewing them as an opportunity to distance themselves from the West and demonstrate Chinese academic superiority over it. But does Song Lihong really mean to imply that Jews are a 'burden' to an academic field, and that an academia without them would be free to flourish? One might also wonder why Song Lihong assumes all Jewish scholars of Judaism to be religious. His work seems to be a misrepresentation of Judaism, and reflects a common misconception within Jewish studies in China that understands Jewish people only through Judaism's religious texts. 'Liturgy,' writes Song Lihong, for instance, 'is a living issue for Jews. Their Jewish prayer book has been read and reread in every generation, in every Jewish community.'[57] This is certainly not the case in some Kibbutz communities, secular Israel in general, the Jewish Autonomous Oblast during the Soviet Union, or Jewish communities before the composition of the siddur. Nor is there a single Jewish prayer book, but different liturgies: historical (First Temple period, Second Temple period, and so on), geographical (Ethiopian, Yemenite, etc.), and confessional (feminist, Reconstructionist, and others).

Current Jewish studies in China often makes the intellectual mistake of trying to understand Judaism and Jewish people only through religious law and practice, rather than through their history of humour, irony, philosophy, and art. As if all one has to do in order to understand Jewish people is study the law as given by God to Moses on Mount Sinai. But how about Heinrich Heine when he says: 'I try to tell my grief and it all becomes comic.' Isn't that Jewish, even if it's not connected to the Jewish faith and studying the law? Or how about Jewish cooking, dances, or Krav

Maga? But somehow there is this notion that everything a Jew does, and thinks, is related to the Torah and Talmud, rather than the product of cultural, historic, economic, or political circumstances in Eastern Europe, Tunisia, New Jersey, or elsewhere. And if this misconception leads to accusations such as Song Lihong's that the Jewish faith stops Jews from conducting academic research within Jewish studies properly, then that is antisemitic.

Other times, it is simply academic narrowness resulting from the general stereotype that Jews are clever bookworms, as if Jews do nothing other than read all day long, and as if through their texts one can understand them perfectly. But one cannot understand the whole of Chinese culture by studying Confucius' *Analects* or Laozi's *Dao De Jing* alone, Iranian culture only through the Koran, or India entirely through the *Bhagavad Gita*. But somehow the understanding persists among many current scholars in China that the way to understand the Jewish people is through the study solely of their religious law. Insofar, the work of these scholars is closer to the 'Talmud' of Korean vending machines than the academic Jewish studies in other places. It's often simply a popular fantasy, an antisemitic stereotype, disguised as 'scholarship on Jews by and for the Chinese'.

6

ANTISEMITISM AND STORYTELLING IN EAST ASIA

When in 2006, actor Mel Gibson responded with antisemitic slurs after being arrested for drunk driving, he later claimed in his defence to have acted badly due to health problems and that he had 'begun an ongoing program of recovery'.[1] Wrongfully, the then head of the Anti-Defamation League, Abraham Foxman, accepted Gibson's request in the interest of helping him with his 'rehabilitation'.[2] By doing so, Foxman 'accepted Gibson's refusal to take full personal responsibility for his words (his anti-Semitic remarks): they were not really his own, it was a pathology, some unknown force that took over',[3] as Slavoj Žižek commented well.

Antisemitism often gets described as some form of 'pathology', as a 'disease',[4] 'disease of men',[5] 'herpes virus',[6] or 'epidemic',[7] not only in public discourse but also in parts of academic literature. Antisemitism is seen here in psychological terms as 'ranging from mild individual prejudice to full-blown exterminationist social pathology'.[8] 'I would call it an intellectual disease,' wrote the historian Paul Johnson, 'a disease of the mind, extremely infectious and massively destructive. It is a disease to which both human individuals and entire human societies are prone.'[9] Comparing antisemitism to a disease at first makes a great deal of sense, as it opens up a discussion about infections, toxicity, mutability, and contagion. But it is, nevertheless, too weak a description, even as a metaphor. It does not explain the rise of antisemitic political movements,[10] nor does it fully grasp the difficulty of getting rid of it, since, as Ruth Wisse observes, 'there is no comparable effort to finding a cure'.[11]

> Those infected with the disease have no strong incentive to seek a cure since they do not suffer the physical consequences; and contrarily, the Jewish victims, who are understandably eager to diagnose the illness and discover a cure, have no access to the carriers and cannot heal those who consider themselves heathy.[12]

The practice of describing antisemitism as a disease has also been criticised for being a mirror image of the antisemitic comparison of Jews with disease.[13] And, more crucially, it undermines individual responsibility. This is highly important. If an action is a symptom of a disease, it is treated differently. Sneezing in front of somebody is morally and legally different to spitting on someone. Or, as psychiatrist Thomas Szasz observes:

> We moderns do not believe in punishing disease or patients for having disease. We do not imprison, much less kill, mentally ill persons; we excuse them of their crimes and hospitalize them ... If anti-Semitism is a disease, then the Nazi leaders were very sick indeed, and the Nuremberg trials were one of the great injustices of the twentieth century.[14]

But, of course, this was not the case. Kenneth L. Marcus argues well that 'the disease metaphor is problematic for the reason that makes it comforting, that is, because it implies that anti-Semitism is wholly foreign to healthy persons in the post-Holocaust West'.[15] Marcus is right when he argues that 'by defining the anti-Semite as an extreme, foreign, virulent other, we create a myth of our own healthy bodies as untouched by this disavowed condition'.[16] Describing antisemitism as a disease or epidemic is, therefore, not helpful.[17] Antisemitism is not the fear of public speaking or the hate of spiders,[18] not a curable illness, and not something one catches like a disease. The mind gets trapped in it, like a disaster, a self-inflicted disaster.

STORYTELLING

Jean-Paul Sartre argued that there is no internal coherence to antisemitism and that antisemitism is a 'passion'. He rejected the notion that antisemitism was an empirical idea, as it does not make any intellectual sense and thus should not classify as an 'idea.'[19] One must agree that antisemitism has never made any sense and never will, yet Sartre was wrong in one aspect: it is not an emotional reaction towards something but rather an ill-guided thought process.

Antisemitism also gets described by some as an 'ideology' or an 'attitude'. It could certainly take on these forms, just like antisemitism can take on the form of a physical attack, a slur, a joke, a movie, a song. Consequently, I propose something rather different, something that takes one to the core of what antisemitism is: storytelling. One should ignore for the moment all the positive things one automatically associates with storytelling. Of course, I'm not referring to fairy tales, Tolstoy, or Hollywood, but a human phenomenon that travels through time and cultures, one that can bring great joy and support our human existence but can also create much suffering and cause the worst of evils. Stories can take on negative forms: fascist propaganda, lies, nightmares. Antisemitism is not a disease that came upon humanity, not always an ideology innocent people fall victim to like joining a cult, but something that gets created, transported, and modified between humans, societies, and time. It is closer to being a dangerous product than a virus or cancer. It is a self-inflicted disaster, a story.

Describing antisemitism as storytelling allows one to simultaneously hold the individual, the storyteller, accountable, as well as recognize the social dynamic antisemitism takes on as it travels between humans across societies, countries, cultures, and history. The concept does not overestimate the individual mind while at the same time does not underestimate social conditions. Antisemitism is a hateful and evil form of storytelling of which Jews (or those perceived as Jews) are the victims. It comes into existence in the minds of individuals before it can spread. It is a story that is whispered at times, screamed at others, politely shared at cocktail parties, preached, or simply thought. It is never right, senseful, elegant, or good, but it always begins as a story. Its existence indicates a problem not just for Jews, but for the entirety of a society or group in which it exists.

But how about antisemitic art and music? Isn't art a story, too, told not in words but in materials, like music is a story told in sound and words? The argument against describing antisemitism as a story would be that it is, of course, not only that. It is something that manifests itself in countless ways, ranging from insults to the murder of millions of Jews. But when we think of the origin, the structure, and the dynamic of antisemitism, thinking of it as a story can be helpful. And in the case of East Asia, a region with almost no Jewish history nor presence, antisemitism for the most part is simply a story about a group of people most East Asians have never been in contact with. It is not an ugly thought or harmful lie told about their Jewish neighbour, co-worker, or son-in-law, but a story about people entirely unknown on a personal level.

Ultimately, the world is a storytelling competition. And maybe stories are all human life is really about. 'God made Man because He loves stories,' wrote Elie Wiesel in *The Gates of the Forest*. We are constantly creating stories with our brain: useful stories, stories of beauty, and stories of evil, which antisemitism is clearly one of. We crave stories because they offer the thrill of change and the promise of meaning. Antisemitism is an ill-guided form of telling people the simplistic lie about how things in this world are changing because of Jews, as well as the false promise that feeling outrage about this will give meaning to their lives. It is not simply a cognitive error but a way of storytelling, as for the antisemite there is often a disastrous pleasure in feeling morally superior to Jews.

The human brain ultimately needs all kinds of stories to answer the question of 'how do I control this chaos?' Of course, antisemitism presents one with a lie, but it still follows the same pattern of storytelling: there is unexpected change, chaos occurs, and, at the end, a 'lesson' of control waits for the consumer of the story. An antisemite may narrate that Jews secretly control world affairs, which would be the cause of the negative change and chaos related in the story, with the resolution being that one needs to learn the 'lesson' on how to fight this unwanted change and control the chaos. This is the evil intention and structure of antisemitism that such descriptions as 'disease' or 'attitude' do not take into account. And the term 'ideology' fails to include those who not only follow an ideological storyline but rather create their own: 'I do this for my career' or 'now I have a reason not to invite her'.

Tellingly, Giovanni Rodriguez called storytelling 'humanity's greatest but most dangerous tool'.[20] Or as the Nigerian novelist Ben Okri writes, 'To poison a nation, poison its stories.'[21] When we follow a story, we respond to it physically via the chemistry of our brain when it produces chemicals such as cortisol, dopamine, and oxytocin. This is powerful, and potentially dangerous, because stories do not need to be factually true for us to respond to them as long as they resonate with our emotions. Even more, stories can distract from facts that don't fit the narrative. Of course, stories can come in any length. The new English translation of Japan's *The Tale of Genji*, perhaps the world's first novel, contains more than thirteen hundred pages, others only three words (for example, Obama's 'Yes We Can'). In the case of antisemitism, this story can be anything between '__ Jew!' to full books, movies, plays, party agendas, and so on. Again, I do not propose that antisemitism is only a story. It is something that creates much suffering in the real world, not just in thoughts. But seeing it as a form of storytelling with consequences in the real world helps one to understand where it is coming from, how it is spreading, and what purpose it serves for the antisemite while it stays and does not go away.

There are poor people who are antisemites and rich ones, mentally ill humans and sane ones, men and women, people with high IQs and low ones, educated and not, people of all ages and backgrounds (even Jewish ones, as cases of self-hate demonstrate), the common denominator being that we all crave stories to make sense of life. Grasping the problem and solving it come from an understanding of where stories come from and how they travel through time and space, adapt to different cultures, and serve bad purposes. Especially in the East Asian context, philo- and antisemitism become powerful stories of fear, ancient history, politics, the search for wisdom, genius, tragic stories of paranoia and of seemingly losing control in a world the antisemite perceives themselves as living in. But how does this typical Western story of a somehow evil group of people, that completely independent of any context exists and controls the world, resonate with consumers of East Asian storytelling?

In his 1932 book *Remembering*, Frederic C. Bartlett beautifully illustrated the problem of cross-cultural storytelling. Bartlett tells of a study in which British participants were asked to repeatedly retell a Native American story called 'The War of the Ghosts' after periods that increased from minutes to months after hearing it. Each time the participants retold the story, they misremembered more and more, while unconsciously changing the story. While 'seal hunting' became 'fishing' and 'canoe' got replaced by 'boat',[22] they more and more started to remove parts while altering other elements of the story, until 'The War of the Ghosts' had become something no longer recognizably Native American, but properly British.

Stories from outside the region do often become uniquely East Asian, too: Buddhism from India became 'Chan' in China and Zen in Japan, which is a Daoist inspired retelling of Buddhism; the South Korean 'Moonies' cult leaders, the 'holy family', were modelled after the New Testament; and the leader of the the nineteenth-century Chinese God Worshipping Society, Hong Xiuquan, who presented himself as the younger brother of Jesus Christ, led the Taiping Rebellion (1850–64). After Japan opened itself up again to the world in the nineteenth century, many stories from the West got retold in Japan, too. Stories about Jews in East Asia are largely copies of imported Western stories.

Philo- and antisemitism remain strikingly familiar in East Asia, as they are believed to teach East Asians a lesson about how the West would work by fixating on Jews. However, something different and important happens with philo- and antisemitism as it is retold in East Asia: its characters and plot remain the same, but its perspective, character judgement, and structure shift.

PERSPECTIVE

But is it possible to generalize the whole of East Asia in this context? Of course, a South Korean person is not someone from China, and someone from Taiwan distinct from a Japanese person. Richard Nisbett, however, put it well in his ground-breaking book *The Geography of Thought*: 'Variations between and within societies, as well as within individuals, should not blind us to the fact that there are very real differences, substantial on the average, between East Asians and people of European culture.'[23] This is especially important in regard to self-focus in storytelling. Western stories are usually told from a single person's point of view, that of a hero acting out their story. Science writer Will Storr calls this 'individualist propaganda'[24] that communicates the idea that one person could change everything. In East Asia, in contrast, the hero is more likely to be a victim of fate, rather than shaping it, while narratives change perspectives and writers have no problem to kill off the main character.

The Japanese political scientist Mushakoji Kinhide describes the Western *erabi* (active, agentic) style as coming from the belief that 'man can freely manipulate his environment for his own purposes. This view implies a behavioural sequence whereby a person sets his objective, develops a plan designed to reach that objective, and then acts to change the environment in accordance with that plan'.[25] The Japanese *awase* (harmonious, fitting-in) style, however, 'rejects the idea that man can manipulate the environment and assumes instead that he adjusts himself to it'.[26] Evidence suggests that feeling in control is not as important for Easterners as it is for people in the West, who associate control over one's life with mental health to a much greater degree. To the Western mind, the world is a relatively simple place of objects one can understand without context and personally control them. A study found, for instance, that Americans regard change as less likely than Chinese people do.[27]

The Western cultural setting of individualism derives largely from Ancient Greece around 2,500 years ago, thanks to its physical landscape. As Storr describes it:

It was a rocky, hilly, coastal place, and therefore poor for large group endeavours like farming. This meant you had to be something of a hustler to get by—a small business person tanning hides, perhaps, or foraging or making olive oil or fishing. The best way of controlling that world, in Ancient Greece, was by being self-reliant. Because individual self-reliance was the key to success, the all-powerful individual became a cultural ideal ... This conception of the individual as the locus of their own power, free to choose the life they wanted, rather than being slave to the whims of tyrants, fates and gods, was revolutionary.[28]

It 'changed the way people thought about cause and effect', writes Victor Stretcher, 'heralding in Western civilisation'.[29] Karl Jaspers coined the term 'the Axial Age', describing the period from the third to the eighth century BCE, during which an explosion of philosophical ideas took place simultaneously but without direct contact, in regions ranging from Greece to India to China.[30] Of course, this timeframe is long gone, and the 'Axial Age' didn't originate all that contributes to societies around the globe today. Should Confucius have been a real person, it is safe to say that he never drank any tea, because it was introduced as a beverage only centuries later (although he might have seen chopsticks, which had just started being used in China during his time). Yet, cultures in Europe and Asia are still highly influenced by this period. The fertile landscape of ancient East Asia, with its rice- or wheat-growing communities, far removed from the situation in Ancient Greece, called for the group to be successful rather than the individual and consequently saw the emergence of a collective idea of the self. In the *Analects*, Confucius describes 'the superior man' as one who 'cultivates a friendly harmony'.[31] While the ancient Greeks saw the individual as the primary agent, for the ancient Chinese it was the group. And while ancient Greeks understood reality as being made up of individual entities, their Chinese counterparts saw reality as a realm of interconnected forces. Consequently, both cultures, with their distinct experiences of life, developed different forms of storytelling.

East Asian stories tend to give characters much more richness. What makes Western stories arguably rather boring and dull in comparison is the expectation on the characters to behave consistently. Western antisemitism follows this pattern, too, as it portrays Jews as having evil intentions as a result of their character, which then leads to negative outcomes for other people, with Jews being evil in a consistent manner throughout all their intentions and actions. Western stories teach us that we can conquer the world if we have just enough courage, that good is good and evil evil, and that everything will culminate in a happy ending. In Japan, however, 'beautiful endings are much preferred to happy endings'.[32] Cultures in the West, however, tend to be individualistic and idealize the victory of a righteous hero who defeats evil, without any morally grey areas.

While the Western tradition emphasises freedom and self-reliance, Eastern thought tends to focus on harmony and unity, and the relationships between things and people. Confucius put emphasis on the '"five relationships" that were the models for all others: sovereign-subject; husband-wife; parent-child; elder brother-younger brother; friend-friend'.[33] This idea is still reflected, for instance, in the traditional Korean concept of a circumstantial nature of morality in which one does not seek absolute fairness or justice but rather to maintain the given hierarchical relationship. South Korea's economic success is even seen by many older South Koreans as a result of these traditional ethics.

A single actor, or small group of actors like the Jewish people, would not be described as having come to dominate the world by their willpower or character alone in a typical East Asian storyline. The focus on the individual as even being able to do so is a deeply Western fantasy. Chinese painter Fan Kuan's eleventh-century landscape masterpiece from the Song Dynasty, *Travelers Among Mountains and Streams* (called by some the 'Mona Lisa of Chinese art'), is an excellent example. Chinese-American writer Gish Jen writes about the painting:

> This is a monumental work almost seven feet tall, in which both the looming mountains and endless deep mists dwarf the miniscule mules and their accompanying human figure, said to be a self-portrait. Fan Kuan's signature to the right of the mule

train, too, is so hidden by foliage that it was not rediscovered until 1958 … the tiny traveler is in any case unperturbed … There is no sense that he needs to be larger or to exert more control over his environment, quite the contrary. He appears perfectly content to be a minute, interdependent bit of a magnificent whole.[34]

Apart from the small size of the human figure in *Travelers Among Mountains and Streams*, the painting may also surprise a Western viewer by its shifting perspectives rather than consisting of a single vanishing point.

CHARACTER JUDGEMENT

The villains in East Asian stories are usually good people who made a misguided choice but aren't entirely evil characters. Of course, there are exceptions. Ryūnosuke Akutagawa—often called the 'father of the Japanese short story'—experimented with Western storytelling when he seemingly retold a fable found in Dostoevsky's *The Brothers Karamazov* with his story 'The Spider's Thread'. The absolutely evil woman of Dostoevsky's version, who had never done anything good in her life except for one time she gave an onion to a beggar, tries to escape hell but falls back into it by the end of the story. In 'The Spider's Thread', we read of a criminal by the name of Kandata who has never done anything good in his life except for one time when he decided not to step on a spider. On his escape from hell, he too fails for eternity.

A character is seen as good in Western stories when they are brave. They rescue, help, defend. In East Asian stories, good characters become good by way of their relations to others; they tend to be portrayed as respectful to the elderly, for instance, or towards other social superiors. In the Japanese 2022 TV series *More Than Words*, when a father confronts his gay son by calling him selfish and stating that his relationship is something he cannot acknowledge, the son leaves. His boyfriend, however, sees how the son's action has caused grief to his parents, and he considers breaking up with him. This is only prevented by a friend's acting as a surrogate for the couple in the hopes of pleasing the parents with a grandchild. A Western viewer might view the boyfriend's behaviour as childish, and perhaps even as weak, running after the parents for their approval. Westerners want to see characters who are true to themselves. But an East Asian viewer would more likely see this behaviour as evidence of maturity and mental strength. In typical East Asian stories, someone reacting with a smile to the insults of their parents shows not weakness but good moral character and strength.

According to stories, Emperor Shun,[35] a legendary leader of ancient China, was forced by his family to engage in degrading labour, to wear cheap clothing, and to eat food of low quality when he was young. Nevertheless, Shun treated his parents with respect until Emperor Yao, impressed by his good character, named him his successor. This stands in stark contrast to the childhood stories of typical Western heroes: Jesus running away from his parents on a visit to Jerusalem to demonstrate his genius by discussing with the elders in the Temple might come to mind (Luke 2:41–52); Harry Potter breaking the rules at Hogwarts; or James Dean in any of his movies. Western stories value independence and strong will and idolize rebellion. They tell of a central and charismatic character who shakes things up, and they are usually told from a single character's point of view. A hero takes charge of an issue and acts.

For an unskilled Western consumer of East Asian stories, it can at times be quite annoying to see reactive characters failing to deliver their own story. But the idea in East Asian storytelling is often to let characters become victims of fate, rather than the creators of it. A single hero is not understood as being capable of fixing the world, and the reader is often confronted with many different perspectives. This is something Western translators of Dostoevsky and Tolstoy have just recently began to understand, too. The contradictions in characters, and the at times chaotic writings of both authors, do not need the translators to 'fix' them. They were intentionally made by the authors, as unusual this is for Western writing. They were not the result of rushed and sloppy writing, but rather meant to show complexities, shifts, and unpredictable actions. This makes more recent translations of these truly innovative writers of the Western literary tradition quite interesting to look into, allowing the reader to discover how well they are often crafted if one only forgets for a moment the common Western expectation of how a story and character should unfold.

Yet, Westerners tend to enjoy stories more if they reflect Western ideas about change, which explains older translations of Dostoevsky and Tolstoy. 'For Westerners,' argues Storr,

> reality is made up of individual pieces and parts. When threatening unexpected change strikes, we tend to reimpose control by going to war with those pieces and parts and trying to tame them. For Easterners, reality is a field of interconnected forces. When threatening unexpected change strikes, they're more likely to reimpose control by attempting to understand how to bring those turbulent forces back into harmony so that they can all exist together.[36]

Unsurprisingly Westerners tend to behave more consistently across all different types of relationships, as Joseph Henrich explains: 'By contrast, Koreans and Japanese report consistency only within relational contexts—that is, in how they behave separately toward their mothers, friends, or professors across time. Across relational contexts, they vary widely and comfortably: one might be reserved and self-deprecating with professors while being joking and playful with friends.'[37] What Westerners might see as hypocritical or 'two-faced', as they expect people to be consistent to themselves, is in the East Asian context rather a sign of wisdom, maturity, and social adeptness.[38] As a Westerner, 'you are supposed to be consistent across relationships, and you will do better socially if you are', says Henrich.[39] This leads to a tendency in the West to view other people's behaviour as a result of their personal traits, regardless of the context. 'He is lazy' would be a reason that he doesn't get anything done, while perhaps the real explanation lies in the context: he might be sick or have had an accident. The antisemitic perception of 'the Jew' to be a certain way (evil, greedy, and so on) is also a result of this Western idea to understand people as consistent across relationships. In this case, Jews would always be greedy or evil because it would be their nature as beings. People in the West are, according to Henrich, particularly biased to attribute actions or behavioral patterns to what's 'inside' others, relying on inferences about dispositional traits (e.g., he's 'lazy' or 'untrustworthy'), personalities (she's 'introverted' or 'conscientious'), and underlying beliefs or intentions ('what did he know and when did he know it?'). Other populations focus more on actions and outcomes over what's 'inside.'[40]

Westerners overvalue the individual as an actor and are rather obsessed with individual intentions, beliefs, and personal dispositions when judging other individuals. And so, antisemites in the West attribute evil intentions and personal dispositions to Jews, and they believe the individual to possess the power to control world affairs. People in East Asia, on the contrary, are less inclined to do so. Japanese people, writes Henrich,

> are less inclined than Americans to weigh intentionality when making moral and legal judgments of strangers, especially in more traditional communities. The application of intentionality in judgment depends heavily on the nature of the relationships among the parties involved. Japan is noteworthy because its formal legal institutions are nearly an exact replica of America's, but those institutions operate very differently because people's underlying psychology is different.[41]

The concept of yin and yang, which is often discussed in Daoism (and to a lesser extent in Confucianism), is another example: the nature of something is always dependent on its context. The calm water of a river is yin; once it crushes down a waterfall, the water is yang. Wheat while it is growing is yang; after it's been cut it is yin. There cannot be a bottom without a top, nor darkness without light. The wheat's roots seek darkness, while its top growth seeks light. Yin and yang complement each other, transform each other. And in regard to Shinto, the Japanese philosopher of religion Iwasawa Tomoko explains that notions of sin are different to Western as they traditionally regard *ara-mi-tama* (the wild soul) and *nigi-mi-tama* (the peaceful soul) to constitute 'two necessary, innate elements of being (i.e., the ebb and flow of vital force in nature)'.[42] While in

Western thought light and darkness, life and death, good and evil, are in conflict, in Eastern thought one would disappear without the other. There can't be beauty without ugliness, nor hate without love. As Alan Watts puts it, these opposites are 'more like lovers wrestling than enemies fighting'.[43]

In the West, philosophy and sciences are mainly interested in 'what' questions.[44] 'What is water?' leads one to the definition of it as H_2O. But water is also something that keeps us alive when we drink it and can kill us if we fall into it; something that lets plants grow and floods lands; something that makes us feel good when it comes out of a shower and bad when it comes out of the sky as rain. It is important for the Western mind to know water's molecular formula, to define its character, to discover what it is, to control it by understanding and manipulating its category. For an Eastern thinker, it is instead vital to understand it as something that flows, changes, and does what it does, not what it is. East Asian thought is, hence, better able to adapt to the object's own spontaneous logic, to withdraw from it or to engage in it, and to generally be more flexible. The ancient Chinese classic *The Art of War*, for instance, recommends something that is rather foreign to the West: 'subjugating the enemy's army without fighting'.[45]

STRUCTURE

Contrary to much of Western military planning, strategy is not depicted in the *The Art of War* as a fixed plan that must be followed from start to finish, nor should victory come at any price. Similarly, Iwasawa Tomoko argues that Shinto cosmogony does not map a path 'from original innocence into chaos, leading eventually, through an essentially linear mode of progression, to redemption and salvation, but rather it signals the recurring and never-ending cycle of order and disorder'.[46] Conflicts in Shinto myths, hence, 'do not resolve themselves into a synthesis'.[47]

The Japanese literary form known as *kishōtenketsu* describes the four-part structure of classic Chinese, Korean, and Japanese storytelling. The word originates as a type of four-line Chinese poem—its Chinese characters refer to the introduction (*kiku*), development (*shōku*), twist (*tenku*), and conclusion (*kekku*)—in which one is invited, in some open-ended way, to search for the harmony between all four parts. There are no simple, clear answers in traditional East Asian stories, as characters are seen as complex, and their behaviours dependent on perspective. Ultimately one has to find answers for themselves in the pursuit of harmony.

Western stories are usually structured differently, the classic Greek example being Aristotle's 'beginning, middle, and end', which would be better described as 'crisis, struggle, and resolution'. Interestingly, children adapt to their cultural narrative remarkably early on. On being spontaneously asked to tell any story, one three-year-old in a study conducted in the United States came up with a perfect series of crisis-struggle-resolution: 'Batman went away from his mommy. Mommy said, "Come back, come back." He lost and his mommy can't find him. He ran like this to come home. He eat muffins and he sat on his mommy's lap. And then him have a rest.'[48] Western antisemitism often follows this mental pattern of crisis-struggle-resolution. Hitler entitled his book *Mein Kampf* ('My Struggle' or 'My Fight'), and the Nazis called the mass murder of Jews so terribly the 'Final Solution'.

By no means am I stating that people at the eastern end of Asia can't be antisemites. Racism and xenophobia are, sadly, very dominant in the region. But people in East Asia do not have the same obsession with ending a story or perceived problem as people in Western culture do, but rather they seek harmony in stories. And their stories tend not to follow the straightforward pattern of cause and effect. In his story 'Yabu no Naka' (In a Grove), Ryūnosuke Akutagawa presents us with a typical Asian way of storytelling in contrast to his experiments with Western styles. In the story, events surrounding the murder of a samurai are recounted from varying and contradicting perspectives: a woodcutter, a Buddhist priest, a released prisoner working for the police, an elderly woman, the accused murderer, the widow, and finally from a spirit medium channelling the ghost of the victim. The story brings into question one's willingness, or ability, to perceive objective truth. In such stories, explains South Korean psychologist Uichol Kim, 'you're never given the answer. There's no closure. There's no happily ever after. You're left with a question that you have to decide for yourself. That's the story's pleasure ... One of the confusing things about stories in the East is there's no ending'.[49] This may explain why East Asians have no problem with philo- and antisemitism existing side by side, which could be seen as different 'true' versions of a story about Jews that function as a paradox without contradicting each other. But, of course, what is seen as 'truth' is a lie in this context, as there is no group of people—Jews or otherwise—that secretly dominates world affairs, the media, and finance.

WHAT A STORY CAN DO

For the past century and a half, East Asia has been flooded with stories and new ways of telling them from the West. In these stories, one could find completely bad characters and entirely good ones, unchangeably being one or the other, with the stories ending in a final judgement and leaving little scope for alternative viewpoints. Naturally, many of those stories did not fall on fertile ground in Asia, but the messages antisemitic stories carried with them intoxicated minds in the region with ideas about 'Jews', even though their storytelling was quite different to local traditions. The region's own local writers became intoxicated too, and the Jews in their stories served to help readers grasp the new world outside East Asia, causing excitement and interest and a sense of novelty (except, of course, for the victims of these stories: the Jews—and the truth).

The tragic upshot is that so many people in East Asia did not come to the understanding that what they had heard of the Jewish people was entirely made up and should not be trusted. But East Asians often believe stories about Jews to contain within them lessons of control and a means of understanding the West, especially in the context of the East Asian tendency to see the West as a 'machinelike society without a human soul,'[50] which Ian Buruma and Avishai Margalit argue in their book *Occidentalism*.

In a world where more and more people feel isolated and without a sense of belonging anywhere, people are dying for stories, dying to feel that they belong, or to relate to anyone, or anything. And people may subscribe to evil stories just for the sake of belonging to something. Antisemitism always seems to find the right places to flourish because it lives off of this human need: Weimar Germany during times of economic instability; Russia after the collapse of the Soviet Union; or even what lies ahead of us, a world of increasing isolation, meaningless work, declining religious and moral values, and uncertainty. Societies must create better stories for people to belong, to relate, to find meaning in life. Unfortunately, there are lots of people, not just in East Asia, who are attracted to the most fantastical stories about Jews in the hopes that they can belong and find meaning in life. (And, luckily, there are many who aren't.) But why Jews? Why aren't Icelandic people the target in these stories, or vegans, or lefthanders? Why aren't the lactose intolerant secretly controlling Wall Street, or Scorpios the White House? Why isn't Marcus Aurelius' *Meditations* full of secret wisdom for these people, or Irish folk tales seen to increase foetal IQ in the womb?

Giving people in East Asia more facts about Jews that prove their common ideas of them to be lies, fantasies, and misunderstandings won't change much if people find personal value and meaning in believing in these stories. A quote generally attributed to Mark Twain comes to mind: 'A lie can travel halfway around the world while truth is still putting on its shoes'. (Ironically, this quote is not actually by Twain himself.)[51] All the facts in the world cannot transform somebody who hates or loves into somebody who doesn't care much. It can quiet somebody for a moment, but it will not change the heart. All the facts in the world cannot change a fanatic into someone reasonable. All the facts in the world cannot change a fixation into ambivalence. Only a story can.

7

BISEMITISM

Antisemitism in East Asia has remained somewhat of a mystery to scholars: 'One of the stranger forms of antisemitism that has emerged in recent years,' writes Steven Beller in *Antisemitism: A Very Short Introduction*,

> has been that in East Asia, most notably in Japan, where there are very few Jews. On closer inspection, however, this antisemitism without Jews shows just how far the status of Jews and thus antisemitism has changed ... What is somewhat different about much of this Japanese approach, however, is that there is more than a touch of admiration of Jews in this attitude, in that Japanese marvel at how such a small group could have such a large amount of power and influence over world affairs. Japanese 'antisemitic' commentators do not so much want to destroy the Jewish 'conspiracy' as emulate the Jews' supposed techniques and strategies of control. While the Japanese are not 'from Mars', it is worth stepping back and looking through their eyes at the Jewish position in Western society ...[1]

But what could Beller mean by viewing it 'through their eyes'? It sounds almost like a justification,[2] as if from the Japanese perspective it could be somehow justifiable, while he puts their antisemitism in quotes. But maybe, with his poor choice of

93

words, Beller pointed to something actually quite meaningful and interesting. What is it that East Asians see, and is it different to the perceptions of other people outside the region? I wonder how antisemitism exists in the minds of those at home in East Asian culture when they look at Jews. By no means am I arguing that East Asians are more antisemitic or less so than people in the West. This book is an argument not in degree but in kind.

To avoid any misunderstanding, when this book continues to speak of 'East Asia', it refers to China and the countries that were heavily influenced by its culture, most notably Korea and Japan. When it speaks of 'Westerners', it means people of a European cultural background. A generalization is possible and meaningful in this context of the study of thought processes behind antisemitism. Similarly, the study of language groups can produce scientific knowledge by generally distinguishing between Indo-European languages and East Asian languages. Of course, putting everything into East/West units without addressing differences in categories such as educational background or gender brings with it the problem to miss the whole picture. Yet, my argument is a generalization because it is meant to give one precisely a general idea of the foundation of antisemitism in East Asia that is fundamentally different in its kind to that of the West.[3]

WEIRD MINDS

In 2010, a remarkable article in *Behavioral and Brain Sciences* by Joseph Henrich et al. addressed Western bias and lack of global diversity when it comes to psychological test subjects, who are normally 'western, educated, industrialised, rich and democratic', or 'WEIRD' for short. In fact, most subjects of psychological experiments are American undergraduate college students making some extra money or course credit by participating in studies on their campus.[4] Psychological research designed to produce knowledge about human behaviour and thought processes 'may have instead uncovered truths about a thin slice of our species—people who live in ... (WEIRD) nations'.[5] This is important, because humans are fundamentally cultural animals, and so cultural differences become psychological differences as well, which inform our different norms and attitudes, our perceptions of colour or even vision in general.[6] But, unfortunately, the scientific literature still remains largely WEIRD[7] and does not adequately address the issue of different perceptions across the globe nor the differences within WEIRD countries.[8] The study of antisemitism is no exception. Its findings are fundamentally on WEIRD antisemites, not on the rest of the world.

In general, WEIRD minds show a greater emphasis on individualism, while the studies on Asians indicate their emphasis on collectivism. WEIRD test subjects also show much higher levels of overconfidence. When asked about their degree of competence, for example, 94 per cent of American professors considered themselves to be 'better than average'.[9] The tendency to inflate self-worth is almost absent in studies with East Asians test subjects. On the contrary, East Asian participants tend more towards an underestimation of their own abilities.

Richard E. Nisbett's book, *The Geography of Thought: How Asians and Westerners Think Differently … and Why*, also helps tremendously to inform our understanding of East/West cognitive differences. He understands Westerners (primarily Europeans, Americans, and citizens of the British Commonwealth) and East Asians (principally Chinese, Korean, and Japanese people) in his ground-breaking research to have kept very different systems of thought for thousands of years. Western thought rests on the assumption that the nature of objects can be grasped in terms of straightforward rules and formal logic by putting them in categories that define what rules apply to the object in question. East Asians, on the other hand, understand objects in their context, which appear more complex to them than to Westerners, while formal logic plays less of a role in solving problems. In East Asian culture, somebody too concerned with logic could even be considered immature. It is, therefore, wrong to assume human cognition is universally the same, and likewise that antisemitism would follow the same mental patterns in East Asia as it does in the West.

This, of course, by no means is to say that one way of thinking is superior to the other. They simply produce different outcomes.

The ancient Chinese understood the concept of action at a distance, which made them understand magnetism and the relation between tides and the moon (something even Galileo did not understand, for instance). They excelled at algebra and arithmetic, while ancient Greeks did so at geometry. Contemporary Japanese are twice as likely as Americans to regard a thing as a substance rather than an object.[10] This phenomenon can be seen in the different medical traditions of both regions as well. The Western analytic, object-oriented tradition seeks to locate a problem in the body and alter or remove it. In the Eastern medical tradition, health is seen as the result of a balance of forces in the body. Overall, East Asians do 'focus more on the relative rather than the absolute'.[11] And so Western infants learn nouns at a more rapid rate than verbs, while East Asian infants learn verbs at a more rapid rate than nouns.[12] Westerners tend to put objects in different categories, while East Asians are more likely to group objects and events in terms of how they relate to one another. East Asians tend to be better at seeing relationships between things but tend to struggle when it comes to detaching an object from its surroundings. Westerners are more prone to making errors by insisting on formal logic, while East Asians are more willing to accept paradoxes in their understanding of this world. Tellingly, Kakuzo Okakura writes in his classic *The Book of Tea* that 'The ancient sages never put their teachings in systematic form. They spoke in paradoxes, for they were afraid of uttering half-truths. They began by talking like fools and ended by making their hearers wise.'[13] When thinking of reality, people in the West tend to see stability, while Easterners assume change. Westerners tend to insist more on one belief versus another, while East Asians are more inclined to seek the 'middle way' when confronted with contradictions. Not surprisingly, antisemitism and philosemitism do comfortably exist side by side in East Asia.

Geoffrey Lloyd argues in his study on the origin of cultural differences in cognition that these two different styles of thinking have been maintained in the West and East Asia since Confucius and Aristotle.[14] This distinction is, however, not an absolute one, as ancient Greece had philosophers like Heraclitus, who proposed paradoxical logic ('no man ever steps in the same river twice'), and

China had philosophers like Mo-tzu or the Ming jia (Logicians) who shared much of the ideas of Western philosophy. But it is in general the Aristotelian tradition that influenced the West, and certainly continues to do so, while the Confucian way of thinking continues in East Asia. Nisbett argues, therefore, that most Westerners

> are confident that the following generalizations apply to pretty much everyone: Each individual has a set of characteristic, distinctive attributes. Moreover, people want to be distinctive— different from other individuals in important ways; People are largely in control of their own behaviour; they feel better when they are in situations in which choice and personal preference determine outcomes; People are oriented toward personal goals of success and achievement; they find that relationships and group memberships sometimes get in the way of attaining these goals.[15]

In contrast, as Nisbett's argument goes, East Asians are generally less concerned with personal goals and are more inclined to maintain harmonious social relations: 'Success is often sought as a group goal rather than as a personal badge of merit,' while 'individual distinctiveness is not particularly desirable. For Asians, feeling good about themselves is likely to be tied to the sense that they are in harmony with the wishes of the groups to which they belong and are meeting the group's expectations'.[16] This must be considered when surveys ask East Asians whether Jews would only think of their own group. The statement does indeed sound antisemitic to a Western listener, but it very well might indicate something positive when stated by an Asian. But it also points to a Western obsession with Jews acting by their own willpower when in antisemitic stories they do bad things because of some evil intention of theirs. In the mindset of the Western antisemite, Jews are in control of their behaviour and seek to achieve something for themselves. East Asians, however, do not tend to value choice as much as Westerners do. (And they do not necessarily feel competent to be decision-makers, as one might encounter it, especially in the United States.) As Hu Shih put it, 'in the Confucian human-centered philosophy man cannot exist alone; all action must be in the form of interaction between man and man'.[17] Attributing evil intentions to Jews, regardless of any context, makes, therefore, less sense to East Asians.

Nisbett's research demonstrates substantial differences between Americans of European descent and East Asians in their dependency on 'analytic' as opposed to 'holistic' ways of thinking. Analytical thinking means to isolate an object—in a way, to 'zoom in' on it—or components of it. By doing so, one gives the object certain properties to explain its meaning, based on strict rules one can then put into distinct categories. Accordingly, analytical thinkers come up with types and their properties, as in 'What type of person is he?—An evil one; A good one; and so on.' They in a way think in straight lines. They have the tendency to believe things to continue according to their type unless this line gets interrupted. Holistic thinkers, on the other hand, focus on the whole and the relationships between its parts. And importantly, especially for this context, they imagine thinkers to follow nonlinear (or even cyclical) patterns. An antisemitic story where 'the Jews' behave continuously in a certain way unless they get stopped is specific to the Western way of thinking.

Since the ancient Greeks, Western civilization has been in a love affair with this idea of stable categories as the basis for discovery, while the ancient Chinese saw the world as constantly changing. East Asians certainly use categories as well, but they are 'less likely to abstract them away from particular objects',[18] as Nisbett argues.[19] Antisemitism could, therefore, flourish in the West in the way that certain bad characteristics are applied to Jews regardless of any circumstances.

Ancient Greek philosophers tended to see the world as consisting of separate atoms, while the ancient Chinese tended to see the world as consisting of continuous substances. If Stendhal is right and 'beauty is the promise of happiness',[20] here classical Chinese thought unfolds its very beauty: in Western Christianity, one is born a sinner; in Hinduism and many schools of Buddhism, the world is an illusion full of suffering. In classical Chinese thought (and especially Taoism), however, the world is seen as a place where everything fits more or less together so that everything can flourish until it declines, and the cycle begins again. The 'Eternal Jew' of Nazi propaganda is in stark contrast to this thought.

There is evidence that modern Asians as well as modern Westerners tend to see different worlds.[21] 'Like ancient Greek philosophers, modern Westerners see a world of objects— discrete and unconnected things,' Nisbett writes, and 'Like ancient Chinese philosophers, modern Asians are inclined to see a world of substances—continuous masses of matter. The Westerner sees an abstract statue where the Asian sees a piece of marble; the Westerner sees a wall where the Asian sees concrete.'[22] The Westerner sees 'the Jew' while the East Asian—not quite knowing what that is—copies the story and applies it to what matters to them: the context. By doing so, antisemitism in East Asia doesn't vanish or become justifiable, but changes in its kind.

In the Western, analytic world, a child performing poorly in a subject like math is likely to be seen as the child lacking in math skills or maybe even as being 'learning disabled'. In East Asia, however, this child would rather be viewed as having to work harder. Or their teacher should be. Or the setting for learning needs to be changed. Compared to people in the West, East Asians mentally organize the world more in terms of perceived relationships and similarities. They have less interest in categories than Westerners and 'find it relatively difficult to apply rules to properties'.[23] This seems to be an important factor when terming antisemitism that applies negative properties to 'the Jews' as a category.

Nisbett's research shows Western parents to be 'noun-obsessed, pointing objects out to their children, naming them, and telling them about their attributes. As strange as it may seem to Westerners, Asians don't seem to regard object naming as part of the job description for a parent'.[24] American parents are much more likely to engage their children in play that involves naming individual toys, whereas Japanese parents are more likely to engage their children in social games such as 'I give it to you, now you give it to me.'[25] Developmental psychologists Anne Fernald and Hiromi Morikawa describe common themes and cultural variations in Japanese and American mothers' speech to infants:

'That's a car. See the car? You like it? It's got nice wheels.' A Japanese mother might say: 'Here! It's a vroom vroom. I give it to you. Now give this to me. Yes! Thank you.' American children are learning that the world is mostly a place with objects, Japanese children that the world is mostly about relationships.[26]

The naming of objects that share something in common leads children to learn categories. Not surprisingly, developmental psycholinguists Alison Gopnik and Soonja Choi found that object-naming and categorization skills develop later in Korean speakers than in English- and French-speaking children they had studied.[27] In their symbolic function, Jews are often a way for East Asians to figure out how they relate to the West and how the West works, while antisemitism in the West is directly about Jews been seen as a negative category one should fight against. The obsession with categories runs through Western (intellectual) history, which antisemitism is a part of, and in fact derived from.

When Westerners see a picture of a small person getting intimidated by a tall one, they are likely to evaluate the scene by attributing character traits to the taller one. He is probably aggressive or nasty, a bully in nature. East Asians, on the contrary, tend to think about the relationship between them. Maybe the big guy is the father or the boss.[28] If asked to name the two related items of a list consisting of 'train, bus, track', Westerners are most likely group 'train' and 'bus' together, as both are vehicles, while East Asians more likely name 'train' and 'track' as going together due to their functional relationship, not their category. But 'If we are what we see, and we are attending to different stuff,' as Henrich argues, 'then we are living in different worlds.'[29] And so do antisemites live in different cognitive worlds in East and West.

RICE THEORY

But why do these differences exist? According to what some call 'rice theory',[30] a region's agricultural history seems to have a lasting influence on its modern citizens' cognition. Recent studies support this idea.[31] While wheat farmers mainly depend on rain fall and do not need to cooperate with their neighbours as much, the labour-intensive process of rice farming requires cooperation to a much larger extent.

This is not only a distinction between Europe and East Asia, as shown by a study that compared Japanese from the northern island of Hokkaido, which was settled by Japanese in a pioneer fashion relatively late in Japanese history, with those from the rest of the country. What the study found was that people from Hokkaido are more independent than those from the rest of Japan. They also demonstrated a more dispositional bias in attribution.[32] On average, people of Hokkaido are less holistic and collectivistic than the rest of Japan.[33] Shinobu Kitayama also found that Hokkaido people are more likely to value personal achievement, independence, and pride than the rest of the Japanese.[34] This is probably due to the late colonization of the island and its agricultural shape, as similar differences have also been found in other parts of the world. Two neighbouring villages in Turkey that concentrated on either farming or fishing as their primary economic activity showed similar differences, for instance.[35] And Thomas Talhelm et al. found thinking patterns appearing to reflect local agricultural conditions by examining twenty-eight different provinces in China.[36] The researchers also asked participants in their study to draw themselves and their friends. People in individualistic regions demonstrated the tendency to draw themselves bigger than others while in collectivist societies they tend to draw everyone the same size. 'Americans tend to draw themselves very large,' Talhelm observed.[37]

Of course, other factors such as age and class do also have an effect as well, and there isn't any black and white when it comes to these questions. But Westerners, and especially North Americans, tend to overestimate their distinctiveness and report themselves as being more unique than they actually are. East Asians are less likely to make this mistake. Cognitive differences also apply to groups of people within the same geographic and cultural context. One of the first studies that compared the cognition of groups within a culture was a 1971 study conducted by Zachary Dershowitz. His study on Jewish Orthodox boys, who have a more interdependent upbringing than secular Jewish boys, found them to show more contextual patterns of visual attention.[38]

SETTINGS AND CONSISTENCY

In the mind that has been trained in East Asia, a person always exists within a setting. Anthropologist Edward T. Hall argues in *Beyond Culture* that the idea that there can be attributes that are not conditioned on social circumstances is foreign to the Asian mind.[39] To the Westerner, it would make sense to see a person as having characteristics that are independent of circumstances, and of moving from setting to setting without scientifically changing their nature. This is the foundation of how 'the Jews' are thought of in a certain way, no matter the circumstances. In the East Asian mind, however, an individual is fluid and conditional.

Philosopher Donald Munro talks of East Asians understanding themselves 'in terms of their relation to the whole, such as the family, society, Tao Principle, or Pure Consciousness'.[40] In my own experience, East Asians seem to have a stronger idea of what it means to be a different person in different settings. The question 'Tell me about yourself!' would most likely lead a North American to give a straightforward answer about their personality like 'hard-working' or 'funny', or their role of 'college professor', or 'I work at a start-up,' or their hobbies, such as 'I go fishing a lot.' These self-descriptions provided by the Western-trained mind are presented very much regardless of context (hence 'the Jew'), while Eastern minds would tend to think in terms of context: 'I'm thoughtful at work' or 'I'm funny with my friends' are more likely responses one would get in East Asia. A study found that Japanese people, for instance, find it very difficult to describe themselves without pointing out a particular kind of situation such as at work, with friends, at home, and so on.[41] Westerners, on the other hand, might find it hard to describe themselves in context to a situation. The Western belief that 'I am what I am' becomes in East Asia more of an 'I am Aiko's friend'.

According to Nisbett, 'there is good reason to believe that Westerners and Asians literally experience the world in very different ways'.[42] A study by Dov Cohen and Alex Gunz seems to back this notion. The study asked participants to recall past situations in which they were at the centre. East Asians tended to describe these situations more from an outside observer while Westerners were more likely to reproduce the situation from their own point of view.[43]

In comparison, East Asians are more skilled at observing relationships between objects and events while regarding the world as highly changeable, complex, and consisting of interrelated components. But, if Westerners focus on objects and their properties when viewing the world, and Asians see the world as objects in context, then it seems reasonable to assume both groups explain events quite differently, too. Westerners with their relatively narrow focus would be more likely to explain events in terms of properties of objects ('the Jew' is __ and does __). East Asians, on the contrary, would be more likely to explain events as being caused by complex and interrelated factors. Westerners are inclined to attribute behaviour to the actor, while East Asians are prone to attribute behaviour to the context. Fiona Lee et al.'s work on sports reporters in Hong Kong and the United States illustrates this quite well.[44] In their study, Americans tended to interpret outcomes of a match as owing more to individual players ('Freshman Simpson leads the team in scoring with eleven goals, but its success lies in its defence.'), while people from Hong Kong understood them more in context ('We were lucky to go in at the interval with a one-goal advantage, and I was always confident we could hold them off. I guess South China was a bit tired after having played in a quadrangular tournament in China.').

These perceptions are not limited to making sense of human behaviour. A study[45] found that Chinese people tend to attribute the behaviour of fish (shown to them in a video) to external factors while American participants attributed them to internal factors of the fish. 'In fact, measurements of eye movements indicate that Easterners make more eye movements and spend less time dwelling on individual targets when inspecting scenes compared to Western participants.'[46] Another study found that Americans and South Koreans regarded an individual's personality as equally important when it came to behaviour, but South Koreans rated situational factors and the interaction between situations and personalities as more important than the American participants of the study did.[47] South Koreans in this study also believed that personalities are more subject to change than the Americans did.

One can, therefore, find that there are in general differences in thought processes, worldviews, and perceptions between the West and East Asia. While Westerners understand the world as being largely static, Easterners see the world constantly changing and personalities as more adaptable. People in the West rely to a much greater extent on personality traits in explaining a person's behaviour, while people in East Asia tend to take situational factors into consideration. And this distinction is important. The Western mind tends to ignore the situation and instead invents explanations for behaviour. A person who gives a fantastic talk to an audience would be seen as a 'confident person', an applicant at an interview perhaps as a 'nervous person', or somebody who attends a party where they don't speak to anybody as 'shy'. The East Asian mind, on the contrary, would be more inclined to consider the context and see the conference the speaker attends as creating an invigorating atmosphere; the interview situation making a person shy in that very moment; or the people at a party not doing their best to include the new guest. One resulting tragedy of Western society is that its people tend to vote for candidates who are good at public speaking, assuming this talent indicates their expertise on the matter at hand. East Asians are comparatively better at avoiding this error and holding off judgement, asking themselves what the situation was the person was responding to. They explain more in context. This is far from the thought process of Aristotle, who explained everything in terms of traits, virtue, or ethics. Good people do good things because they have virtues, so he thought while ignoring the social matrix underlying human behaviour.

Easterners are more likely to see the world in terms of relationships, while for Westerners the world is much more one of static objects that can be categorized, as they so often do

with Jews. In traditional Eastern thought, however, the world—
and reality—is constantly changing and fluid. Hence, concepts
reflecting reality are dynamic rather than fixed. And because reality
is constantly changing, anomalies and paradoxes are continuously
being created, while good and bad, strong and weak, old and
new simultaneously exist in everything. The West tries to avoid
contradictions while searching for principles that will justify one's
belief. Consequently, Westerners seek to appear consistent in their
beliefs. In Taoism, on the contrary, opposites complete each other
and create harmony. As the founder of the Daoist School,
Laozi, put it: 'Tao is conceived as both "is" and "is not".'[48] This is
also captured in the Zen Buddhist dictum that 'the opposite of a
great truth is also true'.[49] Nothing exists in an isolated and
independent way but rather must be understood in its relations,
like musical notes creating a melody in relation to other notes.

DEFINING ANTISEMITISM IN EAST ASIA

Thinking of antisemitism in the East Asian context brings
difficulties with it, as its existing definitions do not seem to
apply properly to the region. The US Department of State writes
that 'while there is no universally accepted definition, there is a
generally clear understanding of what the term encompasses'.
In its 2005 Report on Global Anti-Semitism, the department
defined the term as 'hatred toward Jews—individually and as
a group—that can be attributed to the Jewish religion and/or
ethnicity'.[50] The Anti-Defamation League speaks on its website
of 'the belief or behavior hostile toward Jews just because they
are Jewish'.[51] And Dietz Bering writes that, to antisemites,
'Jews are not only partially but totally bad by nature, that is,
their bad traits are incorrigible.'[52] While Bering is convincing in
his analysis of Western antisemitism, when applied to the East
Asian context this view on antisemitism as something fixed and
existing without any duality is incorrect.

More precise is the International Holocaust Remembrance
Alliance's description of antisemitism, which has been adopted
by the European Parliament: 'a certain perception of Jews,

which may be expressed as hatred toward Jews. Rhetorical and physical manifestations of antisemitism are directed toward Jewish or non-Jewish individuals and/or their property, toward Jewish community institutions and religious facilities'.[53] The historical sociologist Helen Fein includes in her definition additional elements:

> A persisting latent structure of hostile beliefs towards Jews as a *collectivity* manifested in *individuals* as attitudes, and in *culture* as myth, ideology, folklore, and imagery, and in *actions*—social or legal discrimination, political mobilization against Jews, and collective or state violence—which results in and/or is designed to distance, displace, or destroy Jews as Jews [emphasis in original].[54]

In her reading of Fein, Deborah Lipstadt points to the operative word in this definition: persisting. 'It doesn't go away; it's not a onetime event. Though its outer form may evolve over time, its essence remains the same.'[55] I generally agree with Fein and Lipstadt in their take on antisemitism, but the definition fails to capture the East Asian context in which antisemitism can, in fact, simultaneously exist in someone's mind alongside an admiration of Jews. According to Lipstadt, 'This hatred is ubiquitous. It has persisted through the millennia, through different cultures. It has been present in many geographic areas—including those with no Jews in residence.'[56] I agree. However, this definition is not complete either. Antisemitism has been present in many geographic areas, including East Asia, but not in the same cognitive way as it exists in other areas such as Europe, the Middle East, or Latin America. Antisemitism starts in the human mind, and one must take into account that the human mind can function and perceive reality in at least two different ways, depending on which culture the brain has developed in: a Western way of analytical thinking or a holistically East Asian way.

Kenneth L. Marcus understands antisemitism as necessarily persisting as well: 'Antisemitism is a set of negative attitudes, ideologies, and practices directed at Jews as Jews, individually or collectively, but based upon and sustained by a persisting and potentially self-fulfilling latent structure of hostile erroneous beliefs and assumptions'.[57] Similarly, Ben Halpern wrote that 'an "antisemite" is one for whom a tradition of hostility to "the Jews" is activated at a high level as a major and salient element in his identity'.[58] While this may be true in the West, it is not universally true: as the Chinese philosopher Shuchen Xiang wrote, 'the Confucian conception of subjectivity is one that is based upon a process-driven acculturation ... where one responds differently in the evolving situations of one's life'.[59] Antisemitism is, therefore, not automatically a 'major and salient element' of an individual's identity in East Asia, but rather can exist side by side with a positive view of Jews. Therefore, all mentioned definitions of antisemitism are insufficient, as they consider the minds of every antisemite to be linear thinking and Western, and miss the fact that about a quarter of the world's population does not cognitively function this way. This is by no means to say that East Asians are less antisemitic than Westerners, but rather that antisemitism follows different cognitive paths in East Asia, a fact that has been overlooked so far in the field of antisemitism studies.

The image of Jews in East Asia is often a strange mixture of opposites, a blend of hate and admiration, a paradox. As Westerners and Easterners differ in fundamental assumptions about the nature of reality and the world, so does their antisemitism. East Asian antisemitism is distinct to that of other regions, as it takes place in a part of the world that has almost no Jewish history or presence. But people like Erica Lyons are wrong when they make statements such as 'the Japanese didn't really understand antisemitism'.[60] To assume people in East Asia simply copy Western stereotypes about Jews without making up their own mind about it is a mistake. They understand both concepts, both the hatred and the admiration of Jews, they just don't challenge them against one another.

Arguably, East Asians exercise real freedom of thought, which can only exist if one is allowed to hold contrary viewpoints at the same time. And freedom, of course, can be dangerous. They can copy an otherwise foreign type of story: one of single Jewish characters being inherently evil or talented and thus controlling world affairs. But these stories are not just copied; they are consumed and understood in terms of where the East Asian focus lies: the context. An antisemitic story such as 'Jews control the world because they find secrets to do so in the Talmud' would for a Western listener most likely contain the 'lesson' that one must watch out for this allegedly evil group who controls everything, as characters in Western stories are inherently good or evil. For an East Asian consumer who is trained to look for the context, however, the story may posit that reading the Talmud contains wisdom and self-help advice, as has been demonstrated through this example of Jews and control.

Therefore, I propose a different understanding of antisemitism in the East Asian context: one in which antisemitism is in fact fully understood by East Asians, but adherents are accountable based on their unique perception of reality, as East Asian cultures tend to process and express concepts differently to the West. To prevent the further spread of antisemitism, one needs to understand it as a fully developed concept of paradox logic and East Asian culture: not a misunderstanding, not something 'lost in translation', but an East Asian version of antisemitism.

Now, as a Western scholar myself, I do what we do best: categorize the observed to extract meaning from it. *Bi-* implies two parts: bilingual, bipartisan, bisexual, bipolar, and so on. With the term 'bisemitism' I seek to describe a mental state of being flexible to being antisemitic as well as philosemitic, depending on the context. Bisemitism is easily misinterpreted as a kind of experimental phase the region is in, where people out antisemitism at certain times, and at other times philosemitism. But, like bisexuality, bisemitism is a category that does exist; it is not a phase in which one does not yet understand one's own feelings and thoughts. It reflects a lasting mental state of understanding (unless Western ways of thinking are going to dominate East Asia more in the future). When thinking about the problem of antisemitism in East Asia, one should therefore avoid the common confusion and romanticization, and take the problem seriously. Love and hate are opposing but secretly one and the same problem in this context: a problem of an exaggeration, of a fetishization of 'the Jews'. As philosemitism is antisemitism with a plus sign placed before it, they are two different expressions that normally do not mix. But in East Asia they do. One can be both one and the other depending on which context seems more attractive.

8

THE STUDY OF ANTISEMITISM AND
THE WESTERN MIND

When it comes to antisemitism, Deborah Lipstadt knows it when she sees it. 'In fact, there are people, particularly Jews, who eschew definitions and argue that Jews can feel antisemitism in their bones, the same way that African Americans recognize racism and gays recognize homophobia.'[1] Lipstadt refers here to a famous phrase by United States Supreme Court Justice Potter Stewart:

> I shall not today attempt further to define the kinds of material I understand to be embraced within that shorthand description [hard-core pornography], and perhaps I could never succeed in intelligibly doing so. But I *know it when I see it*, and the motion picture involved in this case is not that [emphasis added].[2]

But do we really know it when we see it? The Supreme Court phrase does, indeed, sound convincing, but it fails to recognize that not all humans see things in the same way. Lipstadt, however, argues: 'We should be grateful to Justice Stewart not only for expanding the boundaries of artistic expression but also for giving us this highly utilitarian concept. We may at times find it hard to precisely define antisemitism, but we certainly know it when we see or hear it.'[3] However, there is no general 'I', no 'we', that sees, but there are at least two fundamentally different human ways of seeing and ultimately thinking. Potter Stewart's claim that 'I know it when I see it' is not quite a 'highly utilitarian concept', as a human mind developed in East Asia would most likely see something different than a mind trained in the West. In an interview with *The New Yorker*, however, Lipstadt stated:

> I know it when I see it. Now, that's not a sufficient definition, but it's that way with anti-Semitism. I know it when I see it because these are the elements that are there—something to do with money, something to do with finance, that Jews will do anything and everything, irrespective of whom it harms or displaces or burdens.[4]

Now, what Lipstadt implies here is that there is a way of seeing, of observing antisemitism, should one be its victim. But this is not quite the entire story. It could only make sense if there was only one way of seeing. There are, however, remarkable recent findings that demonstrate how people in East and West perceive the world completely differently. For example, when shown a picture of a little girl smiling while surrounded by sad faces and asked, 'Does the girl in the middle seem happy or sad to you?' Western kids are most likely to answer the question with 'happy'. After all she is smiling, isn't she? East Asian kids, on the contrary, are more likely to perceive her as sad, because they don't automatically isolate the individual from the group to the extent that the Western mindset does.[5] They are more likely to perceive the girl as sad, because the rest of the group is.

While people in the West tend to live in a more deterministic world of salient objects and people, they believe themselves to be able to control events because they understand the rules that govern objects. Chinese people, on the other hand, tend to search for the relationship between things while believing that one cannot understand a part without understanding the whole.[6] Nisbett argues that Easterners 'see events as moving in cycles between extremes; and they feel that control over events requires coordination with others',[7] and that Westerners 'see the world in analytic, atomistic terms; they see objects as discrete and separate from their environments; they see events as moving in linear fashion when they move at all; and they feel themselves to be personally in control of events even when they are not.'[8] This is not only a different conceptual worldview that both groups possess, but they also literally see the world in different ways. This could indicate that East Asians are less likely to single out an antisemite from a non-antisemitic group. This would be wrong, and certainly dangerously naïve at times, but it demonstrates that 'knowing when seeing' is not quite a utilitarian concept for all.

Even within Western cultures, people perceive the world differently on such fundamental levels as the colours they see. Russians, for instance, see two kinds of blue[9] (which might not mean that much, given the precise nature of the Russian language, which also has two different words for cannibalism).[10] Lipstadt (and others) have done an excellent job at describing antisemitism and the results of it, but her idea of 'knowing when seeing' ignores different ways of perceiving the world and antisemitism within it. Underlying this is the assumption that there is only one way to see, to detect antisemitism, ignoring the fact that a holistically trained mind perceives reality differently than the analytical one of Western scholars such as Lipstadt.

But there is another problem with the Western, analytical discourse around antisemitism. While Western antisemites are fanatic about the presumed evil intentions Jews have, others in the West are (rightfully) concerned with the evil intentions of those antisemites. But both are—however completely different they are otherwise—products of the same culture that sees a personal trait as central in coming to a judgement of that person. And so, the debate around antisemitism in the West often appears as a search for labels where people try to talk themselves out. 'I can't be an antisemite, I have Jewish friends/co-workers/neighbours,' and so on.

From a holistic point of view, both of these might be true: one could be a terrible antisemite with a certain person and not an antisemite with one's Jewish friend, just as one can hold homophobic thoughts towards a business competitor but not a beloved aunt. Now, an analytic mind would label such a person an antisemite or homophobe who tries to hide it in other relationships and situations. How else could one be an antisemite except for one's favourite Jewish athlete or comedian? But one could also see this person as someone who is antisemitic in one context but not others. Either understanding could be misused as an excuse for antisemitism, but both ways of thinking about antisemitism are at least possible. This is what makes the study of antisemitism in a region with hardly any Jews so interesting. It reminds one on the flexibility of human thought. We all live by very different stories in different contexts of our lives. Categorizing antisemitism in the sense of 'but Pope Pius XII was no antisemite' can end debates in the wrong way, as both could be true and should be explored: he may have acted antisemitic at times in his life and not at others. While a holistic mind might miss the antisemite within a group, an analytical mind might not notice changes within people and antisemitism within different contexts a person acts in.

The Western field of antisemitism studies should, therefore, not overemphasize its category of 'antisemite' but rather take human action seriously in all its complexity. Antisemitism is not a disease, nor is it a thoughtless passion: it is a story pattern one may follow, or not, in different contexts. It is, unfortunately, a way of thinking and misjudgingly 'making sense of the world'. If the Western discourse around it keeps coming to conclusions of 'He is (not) an antisemite!' in the sense of 'He has the disease!' rather than 'this kind of action or thought is antisemitic!', it will have limited success in disseminating meaningful knowledge on how to prevent these actions and thoughts, in the same way Justice Potter Stewart was wrong in his definition of pornography. The material he was looking at could easily have been art in a museum or gallery and pornographic in a store. Art on its own does not exists without context. 'I know it when I see it in its context' should have been his judgement.

This Western manner of labelling a person or a thing's inherent character does make sense in a culture that expects one to be consistent across relationships and situations. The study of East Asia is so valuable because it makes one aware of the flexibility of thought and personal character. While we tend to label people in the West as antisemites, philosemites, or not, we tend to forget that people can be any of it in different situations, and this is certainly the case in East Asia. Current research by philosophers, neurophysiologists, computer scientists, and roboticists increasingly demonstrates the constant transformation of what we call the 'self'. What can be drawn from personal experience as well is that one can have different versions of oneself in different situations: at work, at home, on social media, dressed up, in the morning, at night, over the weekend, and during the week. We are different when we are hungry or in groups, alone, under the influence of drugs, in nature, or lost in play.[11] Not to speak of the different selves possessed by someone with dissociative identity disorder (formally multiple personality disorder), which can even have different allergies or eyesight.[12] People also have different moralities depending on their state of sexual arousal, which can lead to quite shocking results.[13] In different situations, one is different, sees, feels, and thinks differently. This makes the Western/analytical categorization of people (instead of actions) a rather shaky endeavour in general, which when overemphasized can serve as an excuse for antisemitic behaviour, as with the claim that one can't be an antisemite if one has Jewish friends.

But of course, there are people who remain antisemitic in most or all their interactions, especially in the West, as one expects these traits to be true about oneself, too. Antisemitism is a story one may follow at times, at other times not. But 'the idea that people in other societies judge others based mostly or entirely on what they did—the outcome—violates their [Westerners] strong intuition that mental states are primary',[14] writes Henrich so tellingly. The current field of antisemitism studies seems to be no exception. As such, antisemitic behaviour often gets excused, with people claiming 'she is no antisemite', as if antisemitic is an inherent trait rather than an ill-guided thought process for which one should be held responsible if one displays it. The outcome should matter, not the general characterization of a person. The field of antisemitism studies should keep in mind these limitations of its analytic thinking, lest it not fully come to understand antisemitism as a phenomenon. Otherwise, not only all definitions of antisemitism, but also its research, remain incomplete, remain WEIRD.

CONCLUSION

After decades of stagnation, Tokyo still looks like the world's most prosperous place. In its Shinjuku area, with its bustling, futuristic neon lights, men going on iPad dates with their virtual girlfriends, gigantic manga posters, cosplaying adults, and cafés where guests can pet cats or brush human hair, in one of the safest places on earth, one can dream in public. I could buy a cube shaped watermelon here, cross the street at the same time as 3,000 other people, or join in and daydream of some futuristic innocence.

The invented stories that have been told about Jews in East Asia have come to this, too: somehow innocent and lonely, almost flattering, and potentially dangerous. A mix-up. Whether disease, ideology, or story, one must consider that antisemitism is an evil that is, well, there. Even here. Found in Japanese 'Talmud' publications, coming out of Chinese universities and South Korean vending machines, expressed at Hong Kong protests, and found in Taiwanese hotels and restaurants, it is now everywhere. After all, antisemitism always knows where to come through with its lies and aggression. And people crave lies if they are an engaging story, especially in turbulent and confusing times such as ours. And they crave aggression, of course. That one, too.

I wrote this book because I find the image which many people in East Asia have of Jews to be strangely grotesque, and at times sadly all too familiar. One finds stories of ugliness and hate, and at other times a fetishization of Jews as objects of luck, wisdom, and

117

success. After being introduced to East Asia from the West, these stories became part of local storytelling. But what is cognitively happening here is different to the West, not in degree but in kind. Many East Asians aren't 'lost in translation' but in a story, a terrible, dangerous, ugly one, which might be sometimes perhaps flattering to a Jewish listener if it wasn't so utterly absurd. It is an evil Western story seen from an East Asian perspective. One of admiration and hate. And they come together as one.

Scholarship on antisemitism and East Asian studies are separate endeavours. *The Japanese Talmud* attempts to integrate both fields by using advances in cognitive science and the way East Asians tend to perceive the world differently from people in the West. The argument I make is that antisemitism is not a disease or virus, but a form of evil storytelling. Jew-hate in all its forms is thus global and at times dualistic, not Western and always persistent, and I believe strongly that the next challenge for research into it lies here. Antisemitism, as storytelling, has its roots in our perception of the world, our culture, our cognition. This is where we must look if we wish to solve this dangerous problem. The very fact that antisemitism is cognitively different across the world makes it more complicated, but this may also mean that we are more able to improve things than we think. At least we may influence the flow of antisemitism, instead of seeing it as a disease that needs to be eradicated only to fail over and over in doing so. In the meantime, East Asian antisemitism must be fought better with the law. Singapore may be an example that the wider region should follow, given its relatively low level of antisemitism.[1] One reason for this appears to be effective laws such as the Maintenance of Religious Harmony Act, which takes a radical stance on the punishment of religious offenses.[2]

The Japanese Talmud proposes to understand what is happening as a form of storytelling that in East Asia becomes what I call bisemitic, meaning it can simultaneously encompass anti- as well as philosemitism and is rather unique to the region. Without much of a Jewish presence in East Asia, the other tragedy, however, is not that many Asians believe Jews to be business geniuses or miraculously managing the modern world with their extraordinary talents. No. The tragedy is that they believe that they themselves aren't, assuming themselves to be less than, inferior and smaller compared to Jews. As if being Jewish is an affront to their intelligence and talents, or an automatic qualification for being a guide for the twenty-first century, and as if studying Jews is a way to copy their successes of the past century in this one.

Between university entry exams, insecure employment prospects for those who pass them, high suicide levels, between overwhelming loneliness, confusing cyberspaces, the West still dominating, and them being caught up in all the other struggles and changes this century brings to their region it becomes difficult for many East Asians to understand that being Jewish is simply a different cultural expression of being just another human. This is deeply tragic, as much of the region had not even heard of Jews until relatively recently. And so, it does hold true: the discovery of innocence is its loss. But in the spirit of Shinjuku, one may daydream of a place that still is, where Jews are understood as normal, pure normal, in the middle of it all.

NOTES

INTRODUCTION

1. See, for instance: Stanley Rosenman, 'Japanese Anti-Semitism: Conjuring up Conspiratorial Jews in a Land Without Jews', *The Journal of Psychohistory*, vol. 25, no. 1, 1998, pp. 2–32; Rotem Kower, 'On Symbolic Antisemitism: Motives for the Success of the *Protocols* in Japan and Its Consequences', *Posen Papers in Contemporary Antisemitism*, no. 3, 2006, Jerusalem: The Vidal Sassoon International Center for the Study of Antisemitism, The Hebrew University of Jerusalem; Michael J. Schudrich, 'Anti-Semitism in Japan', *IJA Research Reports*, no. 12, December 1987, pp. 8–11; Daniel Ari Kapner, Stephen Levine, 'The Jews of Japan', *Jerusalem Center for Public Affairs*, no. 425, March 2000.

2. ADL/Global 100. https://global100.adl.org/#map

3. Christopher L. Schilling, 'The Problem of Romanticising Israel–Taiwan Relations', *Israel Affairs*, vol. 24, iss. 3, 2018, pp. 460–6. DOI: 10.1080/13537121.2018.1454002.

4. See, for instance: Sarit Katan Gribetz and Claire Kim, 'The *Talmud* in Korea: A Study in the Reception of Rabbinic Literature', *AJS Review*, vol. 42, no. 2, 2018, pp. 315–50, https://doi.org/10.1017/S036400941800053; Ben-Ami Shillony, *The Jews and the Japanese: The Successful Outsiders*, Charles E. Tuttle Company, 1991; Christopher L. Schilling, 'Jewish Seoul: An Analysis of Philo- and Antisemitism in South Korea', *Modern Judaism—A Journal of Jewish Ideas and Experience*, vol. 38, iss. 2, May 2018, pp. 183–97, https://doi.org/10.1093/mj/kjy002; Christopher L. Schilling, 'On Symbolic Philosemitism in Japan', *Journal of Modern Jewish Studies*, vol. 19, iss. 3, 2020, pp. 297–313. DOI: 10.1080/14725886.2019.1688461.

5. A term used by some to describe the twentieth century. See, for instance, the winner of the 2005 National Jewish Book Award: Yuri Slezkine, *The Jewish Century*, Princeton University Press, 2019 (new edition).

6. The term describes how Asia is expected to dominate in the twenty-first century in fields such as culture, politics, and economics. Although this dominance is by no means set, East Asia does wield increasing cultural influence on the world. East Asians' view of the Jewish people is, therefore, important for the forthcoming development of antisemitism.

7. Robert Sternberg, former president of the American Psychological Association, called Richard E. Nisbett's *The Geography of Thought*, in which he made a similar general distinction between 'Western' and 'Eastern', a 'landmark book'.

8. 'Taiwan Political Activists Admiring Hitler Draw Jewish Protests', *Haaretz*, 14 March 2007, http://www.haaretz.com/news/taiwan-political-activists-admiringhitler-draw-jewish-protests-1.215549

9. Richard E. Nisbett, *The Geography of Thought: How Asians and Westerners Think Differently ... and Why*, Nicholas Brealey Publishing, 2005, p. 153.

1. JEWISH SEOUL

1. This chapter has been derived in part from: Christopher L. Schilling, 'Jewish Seoul: An Analysis of Philo- and Antisemitism in South Korea', *Modern Judaism—A Journal of Jewish Ideas and Experience*, vol. 38, iss. 2, May 2018, pp. 183–97, https://doi.org/10.1093/mj/kjy002. It has been made possible by the financial support of the National Research Foundation of Korea (NRF), the German Academic Exchange Service (DAAD), and the Fritz Thyssen Foundation. I thank the Department of Sociology, Seoul National University and Professor Myoung-Kyu Park for hosting me as a visiting researcher.

2. Ariel Scheib and Mitchell Bard, 'South Korea Virtual Jewish History Tour', *Jewish Virtual Library*, https://www.jewishvirtuallibrary.org/south-korea-virtual-jewish-history-tour; 'Korea (Republic of)', *World Jewish Congress*, http://www.worldjewishcongress.org/en/about/communities/KR

3. Josefin Dolsten, 'What It's Like to Be Jewish in South Korea', *Jewish Telegraphic Agency*, https://www.jta.org/2018/01/30/sports/what-its-like-to-be-jewish-in-south-korea

4. John F. Helliwell, Richard Layard, Jeffrey D. Sachs, Jan-Emmanuel De Neve, Lara B. Aknin, and Shun Wang, 'World Happiness Report', https://happiness-report.s3.amazonaws.com/2022/WHR+22.pdf

5. Yewon Kang, 'Poll Shows Half of Korean Teenagers Have Suicidal Thoughts', *Wall Street Journal*, 20 March 2014, https://www.wsj.com/amp/articles/poll-shows-half-of-korean-teenagers-have-thought-of-suicide-1395300991

6. 'Suicide No. 1 Cause of Death for S. Korean Teens, Youths', *Yonhap News Agency*, 28 April 2015, https://en.yna.co.kr/view/AEN20150428004700320

7. Se-Woong Koo, 'An Assault Upon Our Children', *New York Times*, 1 August 2014, https://www.nytimes.com/2014/08/02/opinion/sunday/south-koreas-education-system-hurts-students.html

8. Ji-seon Lim, 'If You Get Caught Three Times Having a Boyfriend or Girlfriend You Will Get Kicked Out of School', *The Hankyeoreh*, 16 November 2010 (in Korean).

9. Diane Ravitch, 'Why We Should Not Copy Education in South Korea', 3 August 2014. Available at: https://dianeravitch.net/2014/08/03/why-we-should-not-copy-education-in-south-korea/

10. Sarit Kattan Gribetz and Claire Kim, 'The *Talmud* in Korea: A Study in the Reception of Rabbinical Literature', *AJS Review*, vol. 42, no. 2, November 2018, p. 321.

11. Ross Arbes, 'How the Talmud Became a Best-Seller in South Korea', *The New Yorker*, 23 June 2015, http://www.newyorker.com/books/page-turner/how-the-talmud-became-a-best-seller-in-south-korea

12. Ibid.

13. Ibid.

14. David G. Goodman and Masanori Miyazawa, *Jews in the Japanese Mind: The History and Uses of a Cultural Stereotype*, Lexington Books, 2000.

15. R. Arbes, 'How the Talmud Became a Best-seller in South Korea'.

16. Ibid.

17. Meron Medzini, *Under the Shadow of the Rising Sun: Japan and the Jews during the Holocaust Era*, Academic Studies Press, 2016.

18. R. Arbes, 'How the Talmud Became a Best-Seller in South Korea'.

19. The JC, 'Why South Koreans Are in Love With Judaism', *The Jewish Chronicle*, 12 May 2011, https://www.thejc.com/lifestyle/features/why-south-koreans-are-in-love-with-judaism-1.22961

20. R. Arbes, 'How the Talmud Became a Best-Seller in South Korea'.

21. Samuel C. Heilman, 'The Ninth Siyum HaShas: A Case Study in Orthodox Contra-Acculturation', in *The Americanization of the Jews*, New York University Press, 1995, pp. 315–16.

22. Barry Scott Wimpfheimer, *The Talmud: A Biography* (Lives of Great Religious Books), Princeton University Press, 2018, p. 245.

23. Tom Stoelker, 'Discovering Korea Through the Talmud', *Fordham News*, 27 February 2017, https://news.fordham.edu/uncategorized/discovering-korea-through-the-talmud/

24. Sarit Kattan Gribetz and Claire Kim, 'The *Talmud* in Korea: A Study in the Reception of Rabbinical Literature', *AJS Review*, vol. 42, no. 2, November 2018, p. 348.

25. Ibid., p. 348.

26. Ibid., p. 344.

27. Ibid., p. 344.

28. Ibid., p. 346.

29. Erin M. Cline, *Families of Virtue: Confucian and Western Views on Childhood Development*, Columbia University Press, 2015, xiii.

30. Anne Behnke Kinney, ed., *Chinese Views of Childhood*, University of Hawai'i Press, 1995, p. 27.

31. Dave Hazzan, 'Seoul Mates: Are Jewish Stereotypes Among Koreans a Source of Hate, or Love?', *Tablet*, 4 November 2014, http://www.tabletmag.com/jewish-life-and-religion/186194/korean-anti-semitism

32. Scholars on philosemitism repeatedly quote the same four titles: Phyllis Lassner and Lara Trubowitz (eds), *Antisemitism and Philosemitism in the Twentieth and Twenty-First Centuries: Representing Jews, Jewishness, and Modern Culture*, University of Delaware Press, 2008; Alan Edelstein, *An Unacknowledged Harmony: Philo-Semitism and the Survival of European Jewry*, Greenwood Press, 1982; William Rubinstein and Hilary Rubinstein, *Philosemitism: Admiration and Support in the English-Speaking World for Jews, 1840–1939*, Macmillan Press, 1999; and Alan Levenson, *Between Philosemitism and Antisemitism: Defenses of Jews and Judaism in Germany, 1871–1932*, University of Nebraska Press, 2004.

33. See, for instance: Geneviève Zubrzycki, *Resurrecting the Jew: Nationalism, Philosemitism, and Poland's Jewish Revival* (Princeton Studies in Cultural Sociology Book 17), Princeton University Press, 2022; Jonathan Karp and Adam Sutcliffe (eds), *Philosemitism in History*, Cambridge University Press, 2011; Tony Kushner and Nadia Valman (eds), *Philosemitism, Antisemitism and 'the Jews': Perspectives From the Middle Ages to the Twentieth Century* (Studies in European Cultural Transition), Routledge, 2017; David J. Wertheim, *The Jew as Legitimation: Jewish-Gentile Relations Beyond Antisemitism and Philosemitism*, Palgrave Macmillan, 2017.

34. P. Lassner and L. Trubowitz (eds), *Antisemitism and Philosemitism*, p. 7.

35. Daniel Goldhagen, *Hitler's Willing Executioners: Ordinary Germans and the Holocaust*, Alfred A. Knopf, 1997, p. 58.

36. Yaakov Ariel, '"It's All in the Bible": Evangelical Christians, Biblical Literalism, and Philosemitism in Our Times', in J. Karp and A. Sutcliffe, *Philosemitism in History*, 2011, pp. 257–85.

37. Zygmunt Bauman, 'Allosemitism: Premodern, Modern, Postmodern', in *Modernity, Culture and 'the Jew'*, Bryan Chayette and Laura Marcus (eds), Stanford University Press, 1998, p. 143.

38. Marian Mushkat, *Philosemitic and Anti-Jewish Attitudes in Post-Holocaust Poland*, Edwin Mellen Press, 1992.

39. ADL/Global 100, http://global100.adl.org/#country/south-korea/2014

40. Peter Carrier, Eckhardt Fuchs, and Torben Messinger (eds), *The International Status of Education about the Holocaust: A Global Mapping of Textbooks and Curricula*, UNESCO, 2015, p. 75.

41. Quoted in R. Arbes, 'How the Talmud Became a Best-Seller in South Korea'.

42. Sander L. Gilman, *Smart Jews: The Construction of the Image of Jewish Superior Intelligence*, University of Nebraska Press, 1996, p. 6.

43. 'ADL Urges Korean Gov't to Condemn Anti-Semitism Following Pernicious Stereotypes in Media Outlets', *ADL*, 2015, http://www.adl.org/press-

center/press-releases/anti-semitism-international/adl-urges-korean-govt-to-condemn-anti-semitic-stereotypes-media-outlets.html

44. Dave Hazzan, 'Seoul Mates', 4 November 2014.
45. Ibid.
46. Debra Nussbaum Cohen, 'From Left and Right, Why Is a League of Haters Descending on the ADL?', *Haaretz*, 3 May 2018, https://www.haaretz.com/opinion/2018-05-03/ty-article-opinion/.premium/from-left-and-right-why-is-a-league-of-haters-descending-on-the-adl/0000017f-f8ec-ddde-abff-fced79930000
47. Abraham Foxman, 'South Korea's Jewish Problem', *The Times of Israel*, 20 July 2015, https://blogs.timesofisrael.com/south-koreas-jewish-problem/
48. 'Samsung Removes Online Cartoons Mocking Jewish Hedge Fund Founder', *Jewish Telegraphic Agency*, 16 July 2015, http://www.jta.org/2015/07/16/news-opinion/world/samsung-removes-online-cartoons-mocking-jewish-hedge-fund-founder
49. Quoted in: Haviv Rettig Gur, 'Fight Over One of the World's Largest Tech Companies Turns Anti-Semitic', *The Times of Israel*, 9 July 2015, https://www.timesofisrael.com/fight-over-one-of-the-worlds-largest-tech-companies-turns-anti-semitic/
50. Sam Sokol, 'Samsung Pulls Allegedly Anti-Semitic Cartoons From Its Website', *The Jerusalem Post*, 16 July 2015, http://www.jpost.com/Diaspora/Samsung-pulls-allegedly-anti-Semitic-cartoons-from-its-website-409143
51. 'ADL Urges Korean Gov't to Condemn Anti-Semitic Following Pernicious Stereotypes in Media Outlets', *ADL*, 2015.
52. A. James Rudin, 'A View of the Unification Church', American Jewish Committee Archives (1978).
53. Anson D. Shupe and David G. Bromley (eds), *Anti-Cult Movements in Cross-Cultural Perspective*, Garland, 1994, p. 42.
54. Konstantin Asmolov, 'An Unprecedented Level of Anti-Semitism in South Korea?', *New Eastern Outlook*, 25 July 2014, https://journal-neo.org/2014/07/25/rus-neby-valy-j-uroven-antisemitizma-v-yuzhnoj-koree/
55. Donald Macintyre, 'They Dressed Well', *TIME*, 5 June 2000, http://content.time.com/time/world/article/0,8599,2053797,00.html
56. Ibid.
57. Ibid.
58. ADL/Global 100, http://global100.adl.org/#map
59. World Values Survey Association. (2010-2014). WV6_Results_By_Country. Retrieved from https://www.worldvaluessurvey.org/WVSDocumentation WV6.jsp
60. Gi-Wook Shin, *Ethnic Nationalism in Korea: Genealogy, Politics, and Legacy*, Stanford University Press, 2006, p. 2.
61. 'Global Citizenship a Growing Sentiment Among Citizens of Emerging Economies: Global Poll', *BBC World Service Poll*, 27 April 2016, http://www.

globescan.com/images/images/pressreleases/BBC2016-Identity/BBC_
GlobeScan_Identity_Season_Press_Release_April%2026.pdf
62. The McCune-Reischauer system is used throughout this chapter.
63. Emma Campbell, 'The End of Ethnic Nationalism? Changing Conceptions
of National Identity and Belonging Among Young South Koreans', *Nations &
Nationalism*, vol. 21, no. 3, 2015, pp. 483–502, https://doi.org/10.1111/
nana.12120
64. Brian R. Myers, *The Cleanest Race: How North Koreans See Themselves—And Why It
Matters*, Melville House, 2010.
65. John W. Dower, *War Without Mercy: Race and Power in the Pacific War*, Pantheon
Books, 1987, p. 205.
66. Quoted in: Kenneth M. Wells, *New God, New Nation: Protestants and Self-
Reconstruction Nationalism in Korea, 1896-1937*, University of Hawai'i Press,
1990, p. 41.
67. Walter Russell Mead, 'The BBC and "The Jews"', *The American Interest*, 13 May
2012, https://www.the-american-interest.com/2012/05/13/the-bbc-and-
the-jews/

2. LONELINESS AND THE SYMBOLIC VIEW OF JEWS IN JAPAN

1. This chapter is derived in part from an article published in the *Journal of
Modern Jewish Studies*, vol. 19, 2020, Taylor & Francis Group, available
online: http://www.tandfonline.com/10.1080/14725886.2019.1688461;
The chapter became possible with the generous financial support of the Japan
Society for the Promotion of Science (JSPS).
2. Mayumi Asai is a Japanese author. A portrayal of her solo lifestyle appeared
in: Bryan Lufkin, 'The Rise of Japan's "Super Solo" Culture', BBC News,
15 January 2020, https://www.bbc.com/worklife/article/20200113-the-
rise-of-japans-super-solo-culture
3. Matthew Calbraith Perry, *The Japan Expedition, 1852–1854: The Personal Journal
of Commodore Matthew C. Perry*, Smithsonian Institution Press, 1968, pp. 179–
80.
4. Takeo Doi, *The Anatomy of Self*, Kodansha International, 1985, p. 35.
5. See, for instance: Takeo Doi, *The Anatomy of Dependence: Exploring an Area of the
Japanese psyche: Feelings of Indulgence*, Kodansha International, 1973.
6. Casey Baseel, 'In Kyoto, "Hey, you've got a really nice watch" is NOT a
compliment, Japanese businessman says', *Sora News 24*, 27 August 2019,
https://soranews24.com/2019/08/27/in-kyoto-hey-you've-got-a-really-
nice-watch-is-not-a-compliment-japanese-businessman-says/
7. Quoted in: Bryan Lufkin, 'How "Reading the Air" Keeps Japan Running', BBC
News, 30 January 2020, https://www.bbc.com/worklife/article/20200129-
what-is-reading-the-air-in-japan (access date May 4 2020).
8. Quoted in: Ibid.

9. Quoted in: Ibid.
10. Quoted in: Hidehiro Sonoda, 'The Theory of Japanese Culture and the Theory of Reverse Absence', *Japan Review*, no. 12, 2000, pp. 93–104, http://www.jstor.org/stable/25791049
11. Also known as: *nihon bunkaron*, *nihon shakairon* or *nihonron*.
12. Ray T. Donahue, *Japanese Culture and Communication: Critical Cultural Analysis*, University Press of America, 1998, p. 101.
13. Harumi Befu, 'Nationalism and Nihonjinron', in Harumi Befu (ed.), *Cultural Nationalism in East Asia*, Institute of East Asian Studies, University of California, 1993, p. 107.
14. Ibid., p. 109.
15. Roger Goodman, *Japan's 'International Youth'*, Clarendon Press, 1990, p. 60.
16. J. Yagasaki, *Emotionally Becoming 'Japanese'?: A Study of Cultural Identity of Americans Living in Japan*, Unpublished Doctoral Dissertation, University of California, Los Angeles, p. 146, quoted in Ray T. Donahue, *Japanese Culture and Communication: Critical Cultural Analysis*, University Press of America, 1998, p. 101.
17. Harumi Befu, 'Nationalism and Nihonjinron', p. 126.
18. Ray T. Donahue, *Japanese Culture and Communication: Critical Cultural Analysis*, University Press of America, 1998, p. 101.
19. Seiichi Makino and Michio Tsutsui, *A Dictionary of Basic Japanese Grammar*, The Japan Times Publishing, 2020, p. 16.
20. Herbert H. Clark and Eve V. Clark, *Psychology and Language: An Introduction to Psycholinguistics*, New York: Harcourt Brace Jovanovich, 1977, pp. 10–13.
21. Ray T. Donahue, *Japanese Culture and Communication*, p. 101.
22. Richard E. Nisbett, *The Geography of Thought: How Asians and Westerners Think Differently ... and Why*, Nicholas Brealey Publishing, pp. 60–1.
23. Ibid.
24. Ibid.
25. Yuichi Kubota, 'The Infrastructure of Public Opinion Research in Japan', *Asian Journal for Public Opinion Research*, vol. 1, no. 1, November 2013, p. 43; Nisihira, Sigeki, 'Public Opinion Polling in Japan', in Robert M. Worcester (ed.), *Political Opinion Polling: An International Review*, Macmillan, 1983.
26. Hayao Kawai, *Dreams, Myths & Fairy Tales in Japan*, Daimon, 1995, p. 25.
27. ADL/Global 100, https://global100.adl.org/country/japan/2014 (access date 9 October 2020).
28. D.G. Goodman and M. Miyazawa, *Jews in the Japanese Mind*; B. Shillony, *The Jews and the Japanese*; S. Rosenman, 'Psychoanalytic Reflections on Anti-Semitism', *Journal of Psychology & Judaism*, vol. 1, no. 2, 1977, pp. 3–23; S. Rosenman, 'Japanese Anti-Semitism,' pp. 2–32; R. Kower, 'On Symbolic Antisemitism'; M.J. Schudrich, 'Anti-Semitism in Japan', pp. 8–11; D.A. Kapner and S. Levine, 'The Jews of Japan'; C.L. Schilling, 'Japanese Studies in Israel: A Response to Meron Medzini's "From Alienation to Partnership: Israel–Japan

Relation" in the *Contemporary Review of the Middle East*', *Japan Studies Review*, vol. 23, 2019, pp. 143–53; C.L. Schilling, 'Book Review: *Under the Shadow of the Rising Sun*', *Shofar: An Interdisciplinary Journal of Jewish Studies*, vol. 36, no. 3, 2018, pp. 195–204.

29. H. Steven Moffic et al., *Anti-Semitism and Psychiatry*, Springer, 2020, p. 4.
30. David G. Goodman, 'The Protocols of the Elders of Zion in Japan', in Esther Webman (ed.), *The Global Impact of The Protocols of the Elders of Zion: A Century-Old Myth*, Routledge Jewish Studies Series, 2011.
31. Tom Brislin, 'David and Godzilla: Anti-Semitism and *Seppuku* in Japanese Publishing', University of Hawaii, http://www2.hawaii.edu/~tbrislin/David_Godzilla.htm (access date May 7 2020).
32. Ibid.
33. Ibid.
34. Sachiko Sakamaki, 'The Battle for History', *Far Eastern Economic Review*, 23 March 1995, p. 17.
35. Quoted in: Tom Brislin, 'David and Godzilla'.
36. David G. Goodman and Masanori Miyazawa, *Jews in the Japanese Mind*, Lexington Books, 1995, p. 245.
37. Tom Brislin, 'David and Godzilla'.
38. Ibid.
39. Jacob Kovalio, *The Russian Protocols of Zion in Japan: Yudayaka/Jewish Peril Propaganda and Debates in the 1920s*, Peter Lang, 2009, p. 25.
40. Christopher L. Schilling, 'Buddhist Anti-Semitism', *Jewish Political Studies Review*, vol. 31, no. 3–4, 22 February 2021, https://jcpa.org/article/buddhist-anti-semitism/
41. Julian Ryall, 'Japanese Paper Apologises for Anti-Semitic Advert', *The Telegraph*, 8 December 2014, https://www.telegraph.co.uk/news/worldnews/asia/aiwa/11279063/Japanese-paper-apologises-for-anti-Semitic-advert.html
42. See, for example, the Japanese Ministry of Justice website: www.moj.go.jp/shingi1/kanbou_houkyo_gaiyou02-02.html (access date July 8 2020).
43. 'UN Independent Investigator Raps Japan for Discrimination', *Voice of America*, 11 July 2005; 'Japan Racism "Deep and Profound"', BBC News, 11 July 2005.
44. Debito Arudou, *Embedded Racism: Japan's Visible Minorities and Racial Discrimination*, Lexington Books, 2015, p. 3.
45. Ibid. See also: 'Setakachō ryūgakusei haijo seigan mondai: 'Futekisetsu' to shūsei saitaku: Chōgikai honkaigi' [The resolution to exclude exchange students from Setaka Town: A town council meeting adopts an amended version after being called 'improper'], *Nishi Nihon Shinbun*, 21 December 2006; 'Town Opts for Isolation Policy', *Japan Times*, 17 January 2007.
46. See: Sono Ayako, '"Tekido na kyori" tamochi uke'ire o' [Bring them in but maintain an appropriate distance], *Sankei Shimbun*, 11 February 2015; 'Japan PM Ex-Adviser Praises Apartheid in Embarrassment for Abe', Reuters,

·13 February 2015, https://www.reuters.com/article/us-japan-apartheid-idUSKBN0LH0M420150213

47. In 1960, the Japan Association for Jewish Studies (*Nihon Isuraeru-bunka kenkyūkai*) was founded by historians Kobayashi Masayuki, Sugita Rokuichi, and others. Their founding 'Prospectus' stated: 'Publications on the Jews that have appeared [in Japan] in such profusion over the past forty years, including some very recent ones, have combined anti- and philosemitic attitudes in a bizarre melange. It is incumbent upon us to point out that these publications have been all but totally devoid of a basic knowledge of their subject and have been characterized instead by irrational argumentation, anti-historicism, and an aberrant politics based on a form of fanatical racism.' (Quoted in: D.G. Goodman and M. Miyazawa, *Jews in the Japanese Mind*, p. 143.) Despite this brilliant start, unfortunately, not much of academic value of the Association is left today.

48. Ben-Dasan, *The Japanese and the Jews*, p. 133.

49. Ibid., pp. 36–7.

50. An example of this is Hiroshi Ichikawa (University of Tokyo), who sees the Bible as a sadomasochistic report about God punishing the Jews: Hiroshi Ichikawa, 'The Talmud and Japanese Culture', public lecture presented at the Center for Interdisciplinary Study of Monotheistic Religions (CISMOR) at Doshisha University, 7 November 2015.

51. Naomi W. Cohen, *Jacob H. Schiff: A Study in American Jewish Leadership*, Brandeis University Press, 1999.

52. Martin Kaneko, *Die Judenpolitik der japanischen Kriegsregierung*, Verlag, 2008.

53. Ibid.

54. Maruyama, *Nihon no Shisō*, Iwanami Gendai Bunko, 2001. Maruyama's work, even if it is not known by many outside of Japan, is ground-breaking and highly popular in Japan itself. In the spring of 2001, this paperback was reprinted for the 76th time!

55. Hayao Kawai, *Dreams, Myths & Fairy Tales in Japan*, Daimon, 1995, p. 24.

56. Misiko Hane, 'Translator's Preface', in Masao Maruyama (ed.), *Studies in Intellectual History of Tokugawa Japan*, Princeton University Press and University of Tokyo Press, 1974, pp. vii–xiii.

57. Tom Brislin, 'David and Godzilla'.

58. Goodman and Miyazawa, *Jews in the Japanese Mind*, p. 273. The response by Marco Polo's parent company, Bungei Shunju, was, however, surprising and swift. For a description, see: Tom Brislin, 'David and Godzilla': 'The magazine would be completely disbanded. All unsold issues would be recalled. Its editor would be transferred to a non-publishing research section, and its staff dispersed to other Bungei publications. The top officials at Bungei Shunju would take hefty salary cuts as personal penance. One would resign. Officials, editors and staff would attend a series of seminars conducted by the Wiesenthal Center to atone and correct their misconceptions on Jewish history.'

59. For an absolutely brilliant book on the phenomenon, as well as the often-misunderstood history of Shinto, see: John Breen and Mark Teeuwen, *A New History of Shinto*, Wiley-Blackwell, 2010.
60. Goodman and Miyazawa, *Jews in the Japanese Mind*, p. 16.
61. Teigo Yoshida, 'The Stranger as God: The Place of the Outsider in Japanese Folk Religion,' *Ethnology*, vol. 20, no. 2, 1981, pp. 87–99, https://doi.org/10.2307/3773058
62. Ibid.
63. Ibid.
64. Ibid.
65. Toshio Yokoyama, '*Gaijin*: The Foreigner in Japan', in Atsushi Ueda (ed.), *The Electric Geisha: Exploring Japan's Popular Culture*, Kodansha International, 1994, p. 177.
66. Goodman and Miyazawa, *Jews in the Japanese Mind*, p. 17.
67. Ibid.
68. See, for instance: Ray T. Donahue, *Japanese Culture and Communication: Critical Cultural Analysis*, University Press of America, 1998, p. 40.
69. Martin Collcutt, 'Buddhism: The Threat of Eradication', in Marius B. Jansen and Gilbert Rozman (eds), *Japan in Transition: From Tokugawa to Meiji*, Princeton University Press, 1986.
70. Goodman and Miyazawa, *Jews in the Japanese Mind*, p. 20.
71. Joseph M. Kitagawa, *Religion in Japanese History*, Columbia University Press, 1990, pp. 219–20.
72. Harry D. Harootunian, *Things Seen and Unseen: Discourse and Ideology in Tokugawa Nativism*, University of Chicago Press, 1988.
73. *If You Understand the Jews, You Will Understand the Japanese* is based on the antisemitic text *The Protocols of the Elders of Zion*. According to Masami Uno, Ashkenazim are 'fake Jews' who control the world, and that the Japanese, being the descendants of the Ten Lost Tribes of Israel, are going to defeat these 'fake Jews'.
74. J. Victor Koschmann, 'Reviewed Work: Maruyama Masao, Nihon no Shisō Seidoku (An Explication of "Japanese Thought" by Maruyama Masao)', *Social Science Japan Journal*, vol. 5, no. 2, 2002, pp. 267–70, https://www.jstor.org/stable/30209387
75. Ibid.
76. Akio Morita and Ishihara Shintaro, *No To Ieru Nihon* [Japan That Can Say No], Kobunsha, 1989, pp. 42–3.
77. Ibid.
78. Jean M. Twenge, R.A. Sherman, and B.E. Wells, 'Sexual Inactivity During Young Adulthood Is More Common Among US Millennials and iGen: Age, Period, and Cohort Effects on Having No Sexual Partners After Age 18', *Archives of Sexual Behavior,* vol. 46, 2017, pp. 433–40, https://doi.org/10.1007/s10508-016-0798-z; Jean M. Twenge, *iGen:*

Why Today's Super-Connected Kids Are Growing Up Less Rebellious, More Tolerant, Less Happy and Completely Unprepared for Adulthood, Atria Books, 2017.

79. A 2016 Pew study found that, for the first time since 1940, men between the ages of eighteen and thirty-four are more likely to live at home with a parent than with a partner or spouse: https://www.pewsocialtrends.org/2016/05/24/for-first-time-in-modern-era-living-with-parents-edges-out-other-living-arrangements-for-18-to-34-year-olds/st_2016-05-24_young-adults-living-02/

80. William Gibson, 'My Own Private Tokyo', *Wired*, 1 September 2001, https://www.wired.com/2001/09/aiwan/

81. Ibid.

82. Matt Alt, 'The United States of Japan', *The New Yorker*, 4 May 2018, https://www.newyorker.com/culture/culture-desk/the-united-states-of-japan

83. Clay Routledge, 'Suicides Have Increased. Is This an Existential Crisis?', *The New York Times*, 23 June 2018, https://www.nytimes.com/2018/06/23/opinion/Sunday/suicide-rate-existential-crisis.html

84. Nathaniel M. Lambert, et al., 'To Belong Is to Matter: Sense of Belonging Enhances Meaning in Life', *Personality and Social Psychology Bulletin*, vol. 39, iss. 11, 2013, pp. 1,418–27, https://doi.org/10.1177/014616721349918

85. Tyler F. Stillman, 'Alone and Without Purpose: Life Loses Meaning Following Social Exclusion', *Journal of Experimental Social Psychology*, vol. 45, iss. 4, July 2009, pp. 686–94, https://doi.org/10.1016/j.jesp.2009.03.007

86. In 2005, a UN special rapporteur on racism and xenophobia expressed concern about the existence of profound racism in Japan: Doudou Dienne, 'Press Conference by Mr. Doudou Dienne, Special Rapporteur of the Commission on Human Rights', 1 July 2005, https://web.archive.org/web/20120210155802/http://www.unic.or.jp/new/pr05-057-E.ht; in February 2015, Ayako Sono, a former member of an education reform panel, suggested that more foreign workers be imported to meet Japanese labour shortages, but that they be separated from native people in a system of apartheid: Yuka Hayashi, 'Author Causes Row With Remarks on Immigration, Segregation', *The Wall Street Journal*, 13 February 2015, https://blogs.wsj.com/japanrealtime/2015/02/13/author-causes-row-with-remarks-on-immigration-segregation/

87. 'Child Suicides in Japan Hit Record High', *NHK World—Japan*, 13 October 2021, https://www3.nhk.or.jp/nhkworld/en/news/20211013_19/ (accessed: October 27, 2021).

88. See, for example: Elif Batuman, 'Japan's Rent a Family Industry', *The New Yorker*, 31 April 2018, https://www.newyorker.com/magazine/2018/04/30/japans-rent-a-family-industry

89. Ibid.

90. Goodman and Miyazawa, *Jews in the Japanese Mind*, p. 12.

91. The common myth of the origins of the Japanese emperor relates that the imperial family goes back to the sun goddess Amaterasu. Only in 2002 did the Japanese emperor officially declare that, based on historical findings, the Japanese imperial family has human roots in present-day Korea.

92. Tudor Parfitt, *The Lost Tribes of Israel,* Weidenfeld & Nicolson, 2002, p. 159.

93. Quoted in: Shillony, *The Jews and the Japanese*, p. 135.

94. Shillony, *The Jews and the Japanese*, p. 135.

95. Masanori Miyazawa, *Nihonjin no Yudaya Isuraeru ninshiki (Japanese Perceptions of Jews and Israel)*, Showado, 1980, pp. 46–9.

96. Shillony, *The Jews and the Japanese*, p. 137.

97. Quoted in: Shillony, *The Jews and the Japanese*, p. 137.

98. Quoted in: Shillony, *The Jews and the Japanese*, p. 138.

99. Shillony, *The Jews and the Japanese*, p. 139.

100. I am thankful to one of the anonymous reviewers of an earlier version of this text who pointed me to an Israeli writer by the name of Joseph Eidelberg, who also tried to link the Japanese people to a lost tribe of Israel. His argument did not hold water either.

101. Goodman and Miyazawa, *Jews in the Japanese Mind*, p. 39.

102. Jūji Nakada, *Japan in the Bible*, Oriental Missionary Society, Japan Holiness Church, 1933, pp. 133–5. The other examples he saw were: Isaiah 41:2; 41:25; 43:5; 45:6; 59:19; Psalms 50:1; 113:3; Malachi 1:11; Daniel 11:44; and Zechariah 8:7.

103. Kita Morio, *Dokutoru Manbou konchū-ki* [Dr Manbou's Entomology], Chūō kōron sha, 1961, pp. 88–9.

104. Masanori Miyazawa, *Yudayajinron-kō: Nihon ni okeru rongi no tsuiseki* [Theories Concerning the Jews: An Investigation into Debates in Japan], Shinsensha, 1973.

105. Shillony, *The Jews and the Japanese*, p. 142.

106. Goodman and Miyazawa, *Jews in the Japanese Mind*, p. 6.

107. Ibid.

108. Norbert Muhlen, 'The Return of Anne Frank', *ADL Bulletin*, vol. 2, 1957, pp. 1–2.

109. Osamu Dazai, *The Setting Sun*, New Directions Publishing, 1968, p. 158.

110. Quoted in: 'Den Fujita, Japan's Mr. Joint Venture', *New York Times*, 22 March 1992.

111. Henry Louis Gates Jr., *In Search of Our Roots: How 19 Extraordinary African Americans Reclaimed Their Past*, Crown, 2009, pp. 225–41; Hsien Hsien Lei, 'Whoopi Goldberg's DNA Hails from W. Africa', *Genetics and Health*. Archived from the original on 13 May 2008.

112. Jessica Derschowitz, 'Whoopi Goldberg Defends Mel Gibson on "The View"', *CBS News*, 14 July 2010, https://www.cbsnews.com/news/whoopi-goldberg-defends-mel-gibson-on-the-view/.

113. JTA and TOI Staff, 'Whoopi Goldberg Causes Uproar, Saying "Holocaust Isn't About Race"; Apologizes', *The Times of Israel*, 1 February 2022, https://www.timesofisrael.com/whoopi-goldberg-causes-uproar-saying-holocaust-isnt-about-race/ (access date: 8 April 2022).

114. Goodman and Miyazawa, *Jews in the Japanese Mind*, p. 6.

115. Julia Just, 'In Short: Fiction', *New York Times*, 27 December 1992.

116. Masahiko Shimada, 'A Callow Fellow of Jewish Descent', in Helen Mitsios (ed.), *New Japanese Voices: The Best Contemporary Fiction from Japan*, Atlantic Monthly Press, 1991, pp. 1–22.

117. Kita Morio, *Dokutoru Manbou konchū-ki*, pp. 88–9.

118. Norman Cohn, *Warrant for Genocide: The Myth of the Jewish World Conspiracy and the Protocols of the Elders of Zion*, Harper & Row, 1970.

119. Shillony, *The Jews and the Japanese*, p. 224.

120. Christopher L. Schilling, 'Japanese Studies in Israel', Japan Studies Review, vol. XXIII, 2019, p. 150.

121. '60% of Japanese Do Not Trust Political Parties and the Diet—the Majority "Do Not Expect" Political Parties to Solve Issues', *The Genron NPO*, 19 July 2019, https://www.genron-npo.net/en/opinion_polls/archives/5496.html

122. Fritz August Voigt, *Unto Caesar*, G.P. Putnam's Sons, 1938, p. 301; quoted in: Eric Hoffer, *The True Believer*, Harper & Row, p. 90.

123. While the Japanese government and the vast public in Japan do not honour Sugihara Chiune, there are plaques and a museum in his name in the town where he was born, and some of his books and plays have appeared in Japanese.

124. The concentration camp Dachau was liberated by Japanese-American forces of the 522nd Field Artillery Battalion. See, for instance: Masayo Umezawa Duus, *Unlikely Liberators: The Men of the 100th and 442nd*, University of Hawai'i Press, 2006.

125. 'International Convention on the Elimination of All Forms of Racial Discrimination (First and Second Report)', *Ministry of Foreign Affairs of Japan*, June 1999, https://www.mofa.go.jp/policy/human/race_rep1/intro.html

3. TAIWANESE JAIL

1. 'Letter from Chiang Kai-shek to Adolph Hitler, Nanking, September 16, 1936', *The New York Public Library Digital Collections*, https://digitalcollections.nypl.org/items/b8dede36-a489-b668-e040-e00a18063638#/?uuid=b8dee93a-0983-ef8a-e040-e00a1806373a

2. Stein Ugelvik Larsen (ed.), *Fascism Outside of Europe*, Columbia University Press, 2001, p. 255.

3. Robert S. Wistrich, *Who's Who in Nazi Germany*, Routledge, 2013.

4. 'General Alexander von Falkenhausen', *Oxford Reference*, https://www.oxfordreference.com/view/10.1093/oi/authority.20110803095809131

5. See, for instance: R.J. Rummel, *China's Bloody Century: Genocide and Mass Murder Since 1900*, Routledge, 2017, p. 6.

6. Letter quoted in: Jessica Steinberg, 'Chian's Century-Old Support for Zionism Surfaces in Letter', *The Times of Israel*, 10 February 2021, https://www.timesofisrael.com/chinas-century-old-support-for-zionism-surfaces-in-letter/ (access date: 3 May 2022).

7. BBC, 'Taiwanese Dine in Death Camp', 21 January 2000, http://news.bbc.co.uk/2/hi/asia-pacific/610485.stm

8. Christopher L. Schilling, 'The Problem of Romanticising Israel–Taiwan Relations', *Israel Affairs*, p. 3.

9. Ibid., p. 3.

10. Reuters and the Associated Press, 'Taiwan Political Activists Admiring Hitler Draw Jewish Protests', *Haaretz*, 14 March 2007, https://www.haaretz.com/2007-03-14/ty-article/taiwan-political-activists-admiring-hitler-draw-jewish-protests/0000017f-df21-d3ff-a7ff-ffa1b39f0000; 'Taiwanese President's Party Pulls Controversial Hitler Ad', *Haaretz*, 18 July 2001, https://www.haaretz.com/2001-07-18/ty-article/taiwanese-presidents-party-pulls-controversial-hitler-ad/0000017f-e4a5-d7b2-a77f-e7a771090000?v=1680174485857

11. Nitzan Horowitz, 'Israel Slams Taiwan Election Campaign Ads Using Images of Hitler', *Haaretz*, 16 July 2001, https://www.haaretz.com/2001-07-16/ty-article/israel-slams-taiwan-election-campaign-ads-using-images-of-hitler/0000017f-dbb6-d3ff-a7ff-fbb688c40000

12. Ibid.

13. Ibid.

14. Reuters and the Associated Press, 'Taiwan Political Activists Admiring Hitler Draw Jewish Protests', *Haaretz*, 14 March 2007, http://www.haaretz.com/news/aiwan-political-activists-admiringhitler-draw-jewish-protests-1.215549

15. Ross Feingold, 'Sad Old Anti-Semitic Stereotypes', *Taipei Times*, 1 April 2017, http://www.taipeitimes.com/News/editorials/archives/2017/04/01/2003667844

16. JNS.org, 'Taiwan High School Students Stage Nazi-Themed March, Salute History Teacher "Hitler"', *The Algemeiner*, 26 December 2016, https://www.algemeiner.com/2016/12/26/aiwan-high-school-students-stage-nazi-themed-march-salute history teacher-hitler/

17. Ibid.

18. Reuters and the Associated Press, 'Taiwan Political Activists Admiring Hitler Draw Jewish Protests'.

19. Ross Feingold, 'Sad Old Anti-Semitic Stereotypes'.

20. The Anti-Defence League published a press release on 17 November 2011 titled 'ADL Condemns Use of Hitler in Taiwan Ad Campaign', which is

now under password protection at: http://archive.adl.org/presrele/asint_13/3881_13.html

21. See, for instance: Christopher L. Schilling, 'The Problem of Romanticising Israel–Taiwan Relations'.

22. BBC, 'After British Man Abused, Taiwan Debates Its Hidden Racism', 21 November 2015, http://www.bbc.com/news/blogs-trending-34882824

23. Christopher L. Schilling, 'The Problem of Romanticising Israel–Taiwan Relations'.

24. Medzini, *Under the Shadow of the Rising Sun: Japan and the Jews during the Holocaust Era*, p. 155; See also: Christopher L. Schilling, 'Book Review: *Under the Shadow of the Rising Sun: Japan and the Jews During the Holocaust Era* by Meron Medzini', *Shofar: An Interdisciplinary Journal of Jewish Studies*, vol. 36, no. 3, 2018, pp. 195–204.

25. Meron Medzini, 'Hands Across Asia: Israel–Taiwan Relations', *Israel Affairs*, vol. 9, iss. 2, 2015, pp. 237–51, p. 250, https://doi.org/10.1080/23739770.2015.1077603

26. The 'Disclosure Statement' of Sobol's 'From Jerusalem to Taipei: Literature review and future research agenda' (*Israel Affairs*, vol. 29, no. 2, 2023, pp. 290–306) states that 'No potential conflict of interest was reported by the author(s)', and under 'Additional Information' that 'This work was supported by Taiwan's National Science and Technology Council [110-2410-H-032 −001 -MY2].' Taiwan's National Science and Technology Council is the new name for Taiwan's Ministry of Science and Technology since it was reorganized as a new governmental agency in 2022. See: Lee Hsin-Fang and Jonathan Chin, 'Cabinet Postpones Reorganization of MOST', *Taipei Times*, 16 March 2022, https://www.taipeitimes.com/News/taiwan/archives/2022/03/16/2003774885; Is this not a 'a conflict of interest', given that the article reads to me like a press release of the Taiwanese government's achievements? The article is not critical of the Taiwanese government but rather claims Taiwan to be an 'international success story', managing to 'flourish as a vibrant democracy with a strong civil society and a highly developed industry', (p. 294), and that 'Taiwan was capable of implementing major changes within a relatively short time because strong government involvement in society' (p. 296). At the same time the article mentions an author who finds incidents in Taiwan that have been labelled antisemitic as incorrect, without mentioning contrary viewpoints in his 'literary review' (p. 298). And, while one should not romanticize the relationship, are Israel and Taiwan 'twins separated at birth', the article asks the reader. Since Taiwan's National Science and Technology Council is relevant to the research presented in the article, it would have been more appropriate in my opinion for Sobol to mention it in the 'Disclosure Statement' to provide transparency and inform readers of any potential conflicts of interest that might affect the interpretation or credibility of his research findings.

27. Mor Sorbol, 'Revisiting Israel–Taiwan Relations', *Israel Affairs*, vol. 25, iss. 6, 2019, p. 1032. After his controversial article appeared, *Israel Affairs*, however, printed a correction: Christopher L. Schilling, 'Correspondence', *Israel Affairs*, vol. 26, iss. 2, 2020, p. 282.
28. Sorbol, 'Revisiting Israel–Taiwan Relations'.
29. Ibid. Sobol made the claim that Taiwan has an impressive human rights record since it voted in favour of same-sex marriage. This is simply wrong: Taiwan didn't vote in favour of same-sex marriage. It was a court ruling—precisely Judicial Yuan Interpretation No. 748—that legalized same-sex marriage. Moreover, foreigners from countries without same-sex marriage are not allowed to get married in Taiwan, even if their spouse is Taiwanese. Sobol's use of Taiwan's legalization of same-sex marriage as an automatic indicator of a positive human rights record is also unconvincing because it could also been seen as an act of 'pinkwashing'.
30. Schilling, 'Correspondence'.
31. Victor Yong Jen Ong, *China Chooses Israel*, https://www.chinachoosesisrael.org/
32. Victor Yong Jen Ong, 'Correspondence', *Israel Affairs*, vol. 27, no. 6, 2021, pp. 1247–8, DOI: 10.1080/13537121.2021.1993051
33. Jonathan Goldstein, Jewish Identities in East and Southeast Asia: Singapore, Manila, Taipei, Harbin, Shanghai, Rangoon, and Surabaya (New Perspectives and Modern Jewish History), De Gruyter Oldenbourg, Digital original edition, p. vii.
34. These include Marvin Tokayer as well as the former Israeli Prime Minister Ehud Olmert, who was sentenced to serve a prison term for accepting bribes and obstructing justice during his term as mayor of Jerusalem and Israeli Minister of Trade. While he may have been a reliable 'research assistant' in the context of the book, it is not made clear by the author how this is the case. It would have been helpful to demonstrate this clearly in order not to compromise the integrity or accuracy of the book, in my opinion. Also thanked are Meron Medzini, who denied in his writings the genocidal nature of the Nanjing Massacre and Bulgaria's involvement in the Holocaust, called Franco's Spain a 'brave nation', and advocated a conspiracy theory of 'certain anti-Semitic tendencies' (Steven Heine and María Sol Echarren, 'Introduction', *Japan Studies Review*, vol. XXIII, 2019), where Jewish communities would 'open doors in the right places' in their home countries for Israel. See, for instance: Schilling, 'Japanese Studies in Israel', pp. 143–54 and Schilling, 'Book Review: *Under the Shadow of the Rising Sun*', pp. 195–204
35. Ibid., p. 83.
36. Ibid., p. 82.
37. Ibid., p. 83.
38. 2021 Report on International Religious Freedom: Syria', Office of International Religious Freedom, 2 June 2022, https://www.state.gov/reports/2021-report-on-international-religious-freedom/syria/

39. Ibid., p. 98.

40. See the online listing for the Talmud Hotel in Gong Yuan: https://talmud. hotel.com.tw/eng/ (access date 18 January 2020).

4. HISTORICAL MEMORY IN HONG KONG

1. Aleks Phillips, 'Jews in Hong Kong watch cautiously as the city faces the most dramatic protests this century', *The Jewish Chronicle*, 11 November 2019, https://www.thejc.com/news/world/jews-in-hong-kong-watch-cautiously-as-the-city-faces-the-most-dramatic-protests-this-century-1.492932 (access date: February 1 2020)

2. Ibid.

3. Ibid. For a description of Jewish history of Hong Kong, see: Zhou Xun, 'Collaborating and Conflicted: Being Jewish in Secular and Multicultural Hong Kong', in Sander L. Gilman (ed.), *Judaism, Christianity and Islam: Collaboration and Conflict in the Age of Diaspora*, Hong Kong University Press, 2014, pp. 99–114.

4. 'Hong Kong: The Facts: Religion and Custom', Hong Kong government, https://www.gov.hk/en/about/abouthk/factsheets/docs/religion.pdf

5. Christopher L. Schilling, 'Japanese Studies in Israel: A Response to Meron Medzini's "From Alination to Partnership: Israel–Japan Relation" in the *Contemporary Review of the Middle East*', *Japan Studies Review*, vol. XXIII, 2019.

6. Christopher L. Schilling, 'Japanese Studies in Israel', p. 148.

7. Simon K. Li on 'Decoding Southeast Asia's Strange Fixation on Nazi Hate Iconography', *YouTube*, https://www.youtube.com/watch?v=p2TY_pCt7EI

8. On 25 September 2019, protesters announced at a press conference their decision to stop using the term 'Chinazi'. The protests were, however, characterized by their lack of leadership, which explains the continuation of the term being used by protesters.

9. Mary Hui, 'How Hong Kong Protesters Are Defending Their Use of Nazi Imagery', *Quartz*, 26 September 2019, https://qz.com/1715719/hong-kong-protesters-defend-their-use-of-nazi-imagery/ (access date: 1 February 2020)

5. 'JEWS' BY AND FOR THE CHINESE

1. Owyang, Sharon, *Frommer's Shanghai*, Wiley Publishing, 2007, pp. 164–5.

2. Schilling, 'Book Review: *Under the Shadow of the Rising Sun*', p. 202.

3. Ibid., p. 203.

4. Xiao Xian, 'The Chinese People's Knowledge of Jews in the First Half of the Twentieth Century', Aharon Oppenheimer (ed.), *Sino-Judaica. Jews and Chinese in Historical Dialogue. An International Colloquium Nanjing* (11–19 October 1996), Tel Aviv University, 1999, p. 64.

5. Gilya Gerda Schmidt, 'Why the Chinese People Are Interested in Judaism, the Holocaust, and Israel', in Manfred Hutter (ed.), *Between Mumbai and Manila (Proceedings of the International Conference, Held at the Department of Comparative Religion of the University of Bonn. May 30, to June 1, 2012)*, Bonn University Press, p. 259.

6. Xin Xu, 'Chinese Policy Towards Kaifeng Jews', *East Asia*, vol. 23, no. 2, 2006, p. 98.

7. Ibid., p. 93.

8. Chris Buckley, 'Chinese Jews of Ancient Lineage Huddle Under Pressure', *New York Times*, 24 September 2016, https://www.nytimes.com/2016/09/25/world/asia/china-kaifeng-jews.html

9. 'China', World Jewish Congress, https://www.worldjewishcongress.org/en/about/communities/CN (access date 10 May 2020); or 2,800 according to: 'Vital Statistics: Jewish Population of the World (1882–Present)', *Jewish Virtual Library: A Project of AICE*, https://www.jewishvirtuallibrary.org/jewish-population-of-the-world (access date 10 May 2020).

10. Gilya Gerda Schmidt, 'Why the Chinese People Are Interested in Judaism, the Holocaust, and Israel', p. 266. Bear in mind, her study has to be read with caution, as she confuses Taoism with Confucianism throughout the entire chapter and at times writes rather unacademically (For example, 'In many ways, the Chinese dragon and the lion of Judah are soulmates,' p. 266).

11. Irene Eber, *Jews in China, Cultural Conversations, Changing Perceptions*, Pennsylvania State University Press, 2019.

12. Galia Patt-Shamir and Yaov Rapoport, 'Crossing Boundaries Between Confucianism and Judaism', in Avrum M. Ehrlich (ed.), *The Jewish–Chinese Nexus: A Meeting of Civilizations*, Routledge, pp. 49–60; Galia Patt-Shamir, 'Confucianism and Judaism: A Dialogue in Spite of Differences', in Avrum M. Ehrlich (ed.), *The Jewish–Chinese Nexus: A Meeting of Civilizations*, Routledge, pp. 61–71.

13. Galia Patt-Shamir and Yaov Rapoport, 'Crossing Boundaries Between Confucianism and Judaism', in Avrum M. Ehrlich (ed.), *The Jewish–Chinese Nexus: A Meeting of Civilizations*, Routledge, p. 49.

14. Glenn Timmermans, 'Antisemitism by Proxy: China and the Jews', *YouTube,* https://www.youtube.com/watch?v=RzEjRxrkAj4

15. Bei Gao, *Shanghai Sanctuary: Chinese and Japanese Policy Toward European Jewish Refugees During World War II*, Oxford University Press, 2016

16. Glenn Timmermanns, 'Holocaust Studies and Holocaust Education in China', in James Ross and Song Lihong (eds), *The Image of Jews in Contemporary China*, Jewish Identities in Post-Modern Society, Academic Studies Press, pp. 185–205.

17. Salomon Wald, *China and the Jewish People: Old Civilizations in a New Era*, Jewish People Policy Planning Institute, 2004, p. 66.

18. Zhou Xun, 'Perceiving Jews in Modern China', in James Ross and Song Lihong (eds), *The Image of Jews in Contemporary China*, Jewish Identities in Post-Modern Society, Academic Studies Press, 2016, p. 5.

19. James Ross, 'Images of Jews in Contemporary Books, Blogs and Films', in James Ross and Song Lihong (eds), *The Image of Jews in Contemporary China*, Jewish Identities in Post-Modern Society, Academic Studies Press, 2016, pp. 24–36.

20. M. Avrum Ehrlich, *Jews and Judaism in Modern China*, Routledge, 2010, p. 6.

21. Ibid., p. 246.

22. Some of the many examples listed in Ibid. are: Bei Shi (ed.), *The Greatest Businessmen: Jewish Businessmen's Clever Techniques of Making Money* (in Chinese), Dewei International Culture Company, 2003; Bei Shi (ed.), *The Rich Mind of Jewish Merchants: Jewish Merchants' 48 Secrets of Making Money* (in Chinese), Dewei International Culture Company, 2004; Chen Chunfeng (ed.), *Successful Strategies in Business: 9 Key Points on Jewish Success in Earning Money* (in Chinese), Develpress, 2005; Guo Lin (ed.), *The Most Effective Fields of Jewish Business* (in Chinese), Guangdong Economy Publishing House, 2004; and He Xiongfei, *Jewish Wisdom of Family Education: The Cultural Code of the Most Intelligent and Wealthy Nation in the World* (in Chinese), Zhifu, 2005.

23. Ariana Eunjung Cha, 'Sold on a Stereotype in China, a Genre of Self-Help Books Purports to Tell the Secrets of Making Money the Jewish Way', *Washington Post*, 7 February 2007, https://www.washingtonpost.com/archive/business/2007/02/07/sold-on-a-stereotype-span-classbankheadin-china-a-genre-of-self-help-books-purports-to-tell-the-secrets-of-making-money-the-jewish-wayspan/da06370a-5c28-4220-8d4c-cdb03edbc449/ (access date 10 May 2020).

24. *The Jewish Gnomology*, http://product.dangdang.com/9041346.html (access date 10 May 2020).

25. Ariana Eunjung Cha, 'Sold on a Stereotype in China' (access date 10 May 2020).

26. Ibid.

27. Wang Yigang, *Japanese and Jewish Secrets of Making Money* (in Chinese), Guangxi Nationalities Publishing House, 1995.

28. Ge Wenjun (ed.), *Talmud: Jewish Bible on Business and Living* (in Chinese), China Textile and Apparel Press, 2004.

29. Ariana Eunjung Cha, 'Sold on a Stereotype in China'.

30. Quoted in: M. Avrum Ehrlich, *Jews and Judaism in Modern China*, Routledge, 2010, p. 109

31. Ariana Eunjung Cha, 'Sold on a Stereotype in China'.

32. Salomon Wald, *China and the Jewish People: Old Civilizations in a New Era*, Jewish People Policy Planning Institute, 2004, p. 64.

33. Joseph Levenson, *Confucian China and Its Modern Fate—The Problem of Intellectual Continuity*, University of California Press, 1958, p. 91.

34. Salomon Wald, *China and the Jewish People*, p. 65.
35. Ariana Eunjung Cha, 'Sold on a Stereotype in China'.
36. Tuvia Gering, 'Antisemitism With Chinese Characteristics', *YouTube*, https://www.youtube.com/watch?v=jbUqQonUfLg
37. http://qnck.cyol.com/content/2009-01/20/content_2517083.htm (access date 10 May 2020); translation quoted in: Evan Osnos, 'Is China Good for the Jews?', *The NewYorker,* 12 February 2009, https://www.newyorker.com/news/evan-osnos/is-china-good-for-the-jews (access date 10 May 2020).
38. Evan Osnos, 'Is China Good for the Jews?'.
39. M. Avrum Ehrlich, *Jews and Judaism in Modern China*, Routledge, 2010, p. 24.
40. Frank Dikötter, *The Discourse of Race in Modern China*, Hurst, 2015, p. 114.
41. Bei Gao, *Shanghai Sanctuary: Chinese and Japanese Policy Toward European Jewish Refugees During World War II*, Oxford University Press, 2016, p. 11.
42. See, for instance: Avrum Ehrlich (ed.), *Negotiating Identity Amongst the Religious Minorities of Asia*, E. J. Brill, 2009.
43. ADL / Global 100, https://global100.adl.org/#map
44. M. Avrum Ehrlich, *Jews and Judaism in Modern China*, p. 7.
45. M. Avrum Ehrlich, *Jews and Judaism in Modern China*, p. 9.
46. Zhang Shui, *Youtaijiao yu Zhongguo Kaifeng Youtairen* [Judaism and the Chinese Jews of Kaifeng], Sanlian shudian, 1990, p. 1.
47. M. Avrum Ehrlich, *Jews and Judaism in Modern China*, p. 11.
48. Gilya Gerda Schmidt, 'Why the Chinese People Are Interested in Judaism, the Holocaust, and Israel', in Manfred Hutter (ed.), *Between Mumbai and Manila (Proceedings of the International Conference, held at the Department of Comparative Religion of the University of Bonn. May 30, to June 1, 2012)*, Bonn University Press, 2012, p. 260.
49. Quoted in: Ibid., p. 260.
50. See for instance: Ilan Troen, 'Bringing Israel Studies to China', *The Jewish Week* (11 September 2009), p. 29.
51. Meron Medzini, has been invited to guest lecture at universities in China, such as Shanghai International Studies University. See: 'Prof. Meron Medzini', *The Harry S. Truman Research Institute for the Advancement of Peace*, https://truman.huji.ac.il/people/meron-medzini (access date 27 May 2020). Shanghai International Studies University invited him to guest lecture: 'Meron Medzini: China and the Middle East: Promises and Pitfalls', *Shanghai International Studies University*, http://en.shisu.edu.cn/resources/events/lecture/china-middle-east-promises-and-pitfalls (access date 26 May 2020). See also: Shoshana Kranish, 'SIGNAL Celebrates the Work of Renowned Educator, Prof. Emeritus Meron Medzini', *SIGNAL*, 31 October 2019, https://sino-israel.org/articles/signal-celebrates-the-work-of-renowned-educator-prof-emeritus-meron-medzini-2/ (access date 8 April 2023). For a critique, see, for instance: Schilling, 'Japanese Studies in Israel', pp. 143–54; Schilling, 'Book Review: *Under the Shadow of the Rising Sun*',

pp. 195–204; and Schilling, 'The Problem of Romanticizing Israel–Taiwan Relations', pp. 460–6.

52.	M. Avrum Ehrlich, *Jews and Judaism in Modern China*, p. 7.

53.	Fu Youde, 'Distinctiveness: A Major Jewish Characteristic', in James Ross and Song Lihong (eds), *The Image of Jews in Contemporary China*, Jewish Identities in Post-Modern Society, 2016, Academic Studies Press, p. 44.

54.	Ariana Eunjung Cha, 'Sold on a Stereotype in China'.

55.	Song Lihong, 'Reflections on Chinese Jewish Studies: A Comparative Perspective' in James Ross and Song Lihong (eds), *The Image of Jews in Contemporary China*, Jewish Identities in Post-Modern Society, Academic Studies Press, 2016, p. 207.

56.	Ibid., pp. 209–10.

57.	Ibid., p. 211.

6. ANTISEMITISM AND STORYTELLING IN EAST ASIA

1.	Quoted in Kenneth L. Marcus, *The Definition of Anti-Semitism*, Oxford University Press, 2015, p. 51.

2.	Ibid.

3.	Slavoj Žižek, *In Defense of Lost Causes*, Verso, 2008, p. 38.

4.	See, for instance, in Werner Israel Halpern, 'Anti-Semitism, A Disease of the Mind: A Psychiatrist Explores the Psychodynamics of a Symbol Sickness', *Shofar: An Interdisciplinary Journal of Jewish Studies*, vol. 9, no. 1, Fall 1990, pp. 118–9, DOI: 10.1353/sho.1990.0009; Bari Weiss, *How to Fight Anti-Semitism*, Penguin, 2019; Michael Diamond, 'The Anti-Semitism Disease Is Spreading', *The Canadian Jewish News*, 7 February 2020, https://www.cjnews.com/perspectives/opinions/diamond-the-anti-semitism-disease-is-spreading (access date 16 May 2020); Ernst Simmel, *Anti-Semitism: A Social Disease*, International Universities Press, 1946.

5.	Delphine Horvilleur, *Anti-Semitism Revisited*, MacLehose Press, 2021, p. 85.

6.	'Understanding Antisemitism—Deborah Lipstadt', *YouTube*, https://www.youtube.com/watch?v=IXo0-hX4kmk (access date 12 December 2021).

7.	See, for instance: Lenny Ben-David, 'Stopping the Viral Epidemic of Anti-Semitism in the United States', *Jerusalem Center for Public Affairs*, 27 April 2020, https://jcpa.org/stopping-the-viral-epidemic-of-anti-semitism-in-the-united-states/ (access date 16 May 2020).

8.	Kenneth L. Marcus, *The Definition of Anti-Semitism*, Oxford University Press, 2015, p. 47.

9.	Paul Johnson, 'The Anti-Semitic Disease', *Commentary*, June 2005, https://www.commentarymagazine.com/articles/paul-johnson-3/the-anti-semitic-disease/ (access date 16 May 2020).

10.	Steven Beller, *Antisemitism: A Very Short Introduction*, Oxford University Press, 2007, pp. 2–3.

11. Ruth R. Wisse, 'The Anti-Semite's Pointed Finger', *Commentary*, November 2010, pp. 24, 27.

12. Ruth R. Wisse, 'Holocaust, or War Against the Jews?', in Michael Brown (ed.), *Approaches to Antisemitism: Context and Curriculum*, American Jewish Committee and the International Center for University Teaching of Jewish Civilization, 1994, p. 24.

13. Kenneth L. Marcus, 'Accusation in a Mirror', *Loyola University Chicago Law Journal*, vol. 43, iss. 2, Winter 2012, pp. 357–93, http://lawecommons.luc. edu/luclj/vol43/iss2/5

14. Thomas Szasz, 'Letter to the Editor', *Commentary*, October 2005, quoted in: Kenneth L. Marcus, *The Definition of Anti-Semitism*, Oxford University Press, 2015, p. 49.

15. Kenneth L. Marcus, *The Definition of Anti-Semitism*, Oxford University Press, 2015, p. 49.

16. Ibid., p. 50.

17. Nor is it particularly helpful as a metaphor in other contexts. At times, it even reaches levels of intellectual nonsense. Three-time Pulitzer Prize winner, Thomas Friedman, for instance, called 9/11 a 'geopolitical pandemic', the 2008 financial crisis a 'financial pandemic', and climate change an 'atmospheric pandemic': 'Thomas Friedman, Unfiltered', *YouTube*, https://www.youtube. com/watch?v=gBa7wPPBGAo (access date 23 May 2020).

18. The sentence is inspired by a brilliant Jewbelong.com slogan posted on Instagram on 23 December 2021: 'Feel free to hate spiders, and public speaking. But give us a break already. Signed, The Jews.' https://www. instagram.com/p/CX05G1WsN6J/?utm_medium=copy_link (access date 23 December 2021).

19. Joseph Sungolowsky, 'Criticism of Anti-Semite and Jew', *Yale French Studies*, vol. 30, 1963, pp. 68–72, https://doi.org/10.2307/2929258

20. Giovanni René Rodriguez, 'Eleven Things You Should Know About Storytelling, Humanity's Greatest But Most Dangerous Tool', *Forbes*, 30 July 2017, https://www.forbes.com/sites/giovannirodriguez/2017/07/30/ eleven-things-you-should-know-about-storytelling-humanitys-greatest-but-most-dangerous-tool/ (access date 18 May 2020).

21. Ben Okri, *Birds of Heaven*, Phoenix, 1996, p. 17.

22. Frederic C. Bartlett, *Remembering: A Study in Experimental and Social Psychology*, Cambridge University Press, 1995 (first published 1932), p. 67.

23. Richard Nisbett, *The Geography of Thought: How Asians and Westerners Think Differently … and Why*, Free Press, 2003, p. 77.

24. Will Storr, *The Science of Storytelling*, William Collins, 2019, p. 82.

25. Quoted in R. Cohen, R. *Negotiating Across Cultures: International Communication in an Interdependent World*, 1997, United States Institute of Peace Press.

26. Quoted in Ibid.

27. Li-Jun Ji, Richard E. Nisbett, and Yanjie Su, 'Culture, Change, and Prediction', *Psychological Science*, vol. 12, iss. 6, 2001, pp. 450–6, https://doi.org/10.1111/1467-9280.00384

28. Will Storr, *The Science of Storytelling*, William Collins, 2019, pp. 80–1.

29. Victor J. Stretcher, *Life on Purpose*, Harper One, 2016, p. 24.

30. Karl Jaspers, *Origin and Goal of History*, Routledge Revivals, reprint 2011, p. 2.

31. Quoted in: James Legge, *Confucius: Confucian Analects, The Great Learning and The Doctrine of the Mean*, Dover Publications, 1971, p. 390.

32. Hayao Kawai, *Dreams, Myths and Fairy Tales in Japan*, Daimon, 1995, p. 116.

33. 'Introduction to Confucian Thought', Asia for Educators (Columbia University), no date, http://afe.easia.columbia.edu/special/china_1000bce_confucius_intro.htm

34. Gish Jen, *Tiger Writing: Art, Culture, and the Interdependent Self*, Harvard University Press, 2013, pp. 87–8.

35. He is traditionally believed to have lived sometime between 2294 and 2184 BCE.

36. Will Storr, *The Science of Storytelling*, William Collins, 2019, p. 83.

37. Joseph Henrich, *The WEIRDest People in the World: How the West Became Psychologically Peculiar and Particularly Prosperous*, Farrar, Straus and Giroux, 2020, pp. 32–3.

38. Ibid., p. 32.

39. Ibid., p. 32.

40. Ibid., p. 33.

41. Ibid., p. 52.

42. Iwasawa Tomoko, 'Philosophical Implications of Shinto', in Bret W. Davis (ed.), *The Oxford Handbook of Japanese Philosophy*, Oxford University Press, 2020, p. 108.

43. Alan Watts, *Tao: The Watercourse Way*, Pantheon, 1977, p. 23.

44. Roel Sterckx, *Ways of Heaven: An Introduction to Chinese Thought*, Basic Books, 2019, pp. 72–3.

45. Sun Tzu Ping Fa and R.D. Sawyer, *The Art of War: Sun-Tzu Ping Fa*, Westview Press, 1994, Chapter 3.

46. Iwasawa Tomoko, 'Philosophical Implications of Shinto', p. 108.

47. Ibid.

48. Quoted in Jonathan Gottschall, *The Storytelling Animal*, HMH Books, 2012, p. 33.

49. Quoted in Will Storr, *The Science of Storytelling*, William Collins, 2019, p. 83.

50. Ian Buruma and Avishai Margalit, *Occidentalism: The West in the Eyes of Its Enemies*, Penguin Press, 2004, p. 9.

51. *The Yale Book of Quotations* (Fred R. Shapiro [ed.], *The Yale Book of Quotations*, Yale University Press, 2006, p. 615) has the following entry: '"A lie will go round the world while truth is pulling its boots on." C. H. Spurgeon, *Gems from Spurgeon* (1859).' An earlier version appears in the *Portland (Me.) Gazette*,

5 September 1820: 'Falsehood will fly from Maine to Georgia, while truth is pulling her boots on.' Still earlier, Jonathan Swift wrote in *The Examiner*, 9 November 1710: 'Falsehood flies, and the truth comes limping after it.'

7. BISEMITISM

1. Steven Beller, *Antisemitism: A Very Short Introduction*, Oxford University Press, 2007, pp. 109–10.
2. Beller's entire section on Japan seems, unfortunately, in serious need of refinement in my opinion. See, for instance, page 110: 'Given the human inclination to explain one's own problems by the unfair advantages taken by others, what is remarkable about Jews and antisemitism in the world today is not how much antisemitic sentiment and prejudice remains in Western societies, but how little.'
3. Robert Sternberg, former president of the American Psychological Association, called Richard E. Nisbett's *The Geography of Thought*, in which he made a similar general distinction between 'Western' and 'Eastern', a 'landmark book'. See: https://www.simonandschuster.com/books/The-Geography-of-Thought/Richard-Nisbett/9780743255356
4. Joseph Henrich, Steven J. Heine, and Ara Norenzayan, 'The weirdest people in the world?', *Behavioral and Brain Sciences*, vol. 33, nos. 2–3, 2010, pp. 61–83, DOI: 10.1017/S0140525X0999152X
5. Michael Muthukrishna, Adrian V. Bell, Joseph Henrich, et al., 'Beyond Western, Educated, Industrial, Rich, and Democratic (WEIRD) Psychology: Measuring and Mapping Scales of Cultural and Psychological Distance', *Psychological Science*, vol. 31, no. 6, 2020, pp. 678–701, https://doi.org/10.1177/09567976209167; See also: Henrich, Heine, and Norenzayan, 'The weirdest people in the world?'.
6. Michele Gelfand, *Rule makers, Rule Breakers: Tight and Loose Cultures and the Secret Signals That Direct Our Lives*, Scribner, 2019; Robert Boyd, *A Different Kind of Animal: How Culture Transformed Our Species*, Princeton University Press, 2017.
7. Mostafa Salari Rad, Alison Jane Martingano, and Jeremy Ginges, 'Toward a Psychology of *Homo Sapiens*: Making Psychological Science More Representative of the Human Population', *Proceedings of the National Academy of Sciences*, vol. 115, no. 45, pp. 11401–5, https://www.pnas.org/doi/full/10.1073/pnas.1721165115
8. Henrich, Heine, and Norenzayan, 'The weirdest people in the world?', Robert R. McCrae, Antonio Terracciano, and 79 Members of the Personality Profiles of Cultures Project, 'Personality Profiles of Cultures: Aggregate Personality Traits', *Journal of Personality and Social Psychology*, vol. 89, no. 3, 2005, pp. 407–425, DOI: 10.1037/0022-3514.89.3.407; Muthukrishna, Bell, Henrich, et al., 'Beyond Western, Educated, Industrial, Rich, and Democratic (WEIRD) Psychology'.

9. Samuel C. Karpen, 'The Social Psychology of Biased Self-Assessment', *American Journal of Pharmaceutical Education*, vol. 82, no. 5, June 2018, pp. 6, 299, DOI: 10.5688/ajpe6299

10. Richard E. Nisbett, *The Geography of Thought*, p. 192.

11. Shinobu Kitayama, Sean Duffy, Tadashi Kawamura and Jeff T. Larsen, 'Perceiving an Object and Its Context in Different Cultures: A Cultural Look at the New Look', *Psychological Science*, vol. 14, no. 3, 2003, pp. 201–6, DOI: 10.1111/1467-9280.02432

12. Richard E. Nisbett, *The Geography of Thought*, p. xix.

13. Kakuzo Okakura, *The Book of Tea*, Shambala, 2003, p. 34.

14. Geoffrey E.R. Lloyd, 'Science in Antiquity: The Greek and Chinese cases and Their Relevance to the Problems of Culture and Cognition', in David R. Olson and Nancy Torrance (eds), *Modes of Thought: Explorations in Culture and Cognition*, Cambridge University Press, 1996, pp. 15–33.

15. Richard E. Nisbett, *The Geography of Thought*, pp. 47–8.

16. Richard E. Nisbett, *The Geography of Thought*, p. 49.

17. H. Shih, *Chung-kuo che-hsueh shi ta-kang* [An Outline of the History of Chinese Philosophy], Commercial Press, 1919.

18. Richard E. Nisbett, *The Geography of Thought*, p. 153.

19. Ibid.

20. Quoted in: Alain de Botton, *The Architecture of Happiness*, reprint edition, Vintage, 2008, p. 98.

21. See, for instance: Mutsumi Imai and Dedre Gentner, 'A Cross-Linguistic Study of Early Word Meaning: Universal Ontology and Linguistic Influence', *Cognition*, vol. 62, no. 2, 1997, pp. 169–200, DOI: 10.1016/s0010-0277(96)00784-6

22. Richard E. Nisbett, *The Geography of Thought*, p. 82.

23. Richard E. Nisbett, *The Geography of Thought*, p. 148.

24. Richard E. Nisbett, *The Geography of Thought*, p. 150.

25. Anne Fernald and Hiromi Morikawa, 'Common Themes and Cultural Variations in Japanese and American Mothers' Speech to Infants', *Child Development*, vol. 64, no. 3, 1993, pp. 637–56, https://pubmed.ncbi.nlm.nih.gov/8339686/

26. Ibid.

27. Alison Gopnik and Soonja Choi, 'Do Linguistic Differences Lead to Cognitive Differences? A Cross-Linguistic Study of Semantic and Cognitive Development', *First Language*, vol. 10, iss. 30, 1990, pp. 199–215, https://doi.org/10.1177/014272379001003002

28. David Robson, 'How East and West Think in Profoundly Different Ways', BBC, 19 January 2017, https://www.bbc.com/future/article/20170118-how-east-and-west-think-in-profoundly-different-ways

29. Ibid.

30. Thomas Talhelm, Xuemin Zhang, Shigehiro Oishi, Shimen Chen, et al., 'Large-Scale Psychological Differences Within China Explained by Rice Versus Wheat

Agriculture', *Science*, vol. 344, iss. 6184, 2014, pp. 603–8, DOI: 10.1126/science.1246850; Joseph Henrich, 'Rice, Psychology, and Innovation', *Science*, vol. 344, iss. 6184, 2014, pp. 593–4, DOI: 10.1126/science.1253815

31. Thomas Talhelm, Xuemin Zhang, Shigehiro Oishi, Shimen Chen, et al., 'Large-Scale Psychological Differences Within China Explained by Rice Versus Wheat Agriculture'; Joseph Henrich, 'Rice, Psychology, and Innovation'.

32. Shinobu Kitayama, Keiko Ishii, Toshie Imada, Kosuke Takemura, and Jenny Ramaswamy, 'Voluntary Settlement and the Spirit of Independence: Evidence From Japan's "Northern Frontier"', *Journal of Personality and Social Psychology*, vol. 91, 2006, pp. 369–84.

33. Ayse K. Uskul, Shinobu Kitayama, and Richard E. Nisbett, 'Ecocultural Basis of Cognition: Farmers and Fishermen Are More Holistic Than Herders', *Proceedings of the National Academy of Sciences of the United States of America*, vol. 105, no. 25, June 2008, pp. 8552–6, https://doi.org/10.1073/pnas.0803874105

34. David Robson, 'How East and West Think in Profoundly Different Ways'.

35. Uskul, A.K., Kitayama, S., & Nisbett, R.E., 'Ecocultural basis of cognition: Farmers and fishermen are more holistic than herders'.

36. Talhelm, T., Zhang, X., Oishi, S., Shimin, C., Duan, D., Lan, X., et al., 'Largescale psychological differences within China explained by rice versus wheat agriculture'.

37. David Robson, 'How East and West Think in Profoundly Different Ways'.

38. Zachary Dershowitz, 'Jewish Sub-Cultural Patterns and Psychological Differentiation', *Journal of International Psychology*, vol. 6, iss. 3, 1971, pp. 223–31, https://doi.org/10.1080/00207597108246686

39. Edward T. Hall, *Beyond Culture*, Anchor Books, 1976.

40. Donald Munro, 'Introduction', in Donald Munro (ed.), *Individualism and Holism: Studies in Confucian and Taoist Values*, Center for Chinese Studies, University of Michigan, 1985, pp. 1–34.

41. Steven D. Cousins, 'Culture and Self-Perception in Japan and the United States', *Journal of Personality and Social Psychology*, vol. 56, no. 1, 1989, pp. 124–31, https://doi.org/10.1037/0022-3514.56.1.124; see also Manford H. Kuhn and Thomas S. McPartland, 'An Empirical Investigation of Self-Attitudes', *American Sociological Review*, vol. 19, no. 1, 1954, pp. 68–76, https://doi.org/10.2307/2088175

42. Richard E. Nisbett, *The Geography of Thought*, p. 87.

43. Dov Cohen and Alex Gunz, 'As Seen by the Other …: Perspectives on the Self in the Memories and Emotional Perceptions of Easterners and Westerners', *Psychological Science*, vol. 13, no. 1, 2002, pp. 55–9, https://doi.org/10.1111/1467-9280.00409

44. Fiona Lee, Mark Hallahan, and Thaddeus A. Herzog, 'Explaining Real Life Events: How Culture and Domain Shape Attributions', *Personality*

and Social Psychology Bulletin, vol. 22, no. 7, 1996, pp. 732–41, DOI: 10.1177/0146167296227007

45. Michael W. Morris, and Kaiping Peng, 'Culture and Cause: American and Chinese Attributions for Social and Physical Events', *Journal of Personality and Social Psychology*, vol. 67, no. 6, 1994, pp. 949–71, DOI: 10.1037//0022-3514.67.6.949

46. Hannah Faye Chua, Julie E. Boland, and Richard E. Nisbett, 'Cultural Variation in Eye Movements During Scene Perception', *Proceedings of the National Academy of Sciences of the United States of America*, vol. 102, no. 35, 2005, pp. 12629–33, https://doi.org/10.1073/pnas.0506162102

47. Ara Norenzayan, Incheol Choi, and Richard E. Nisbett, 'Cultural Similarities and Differences in Social Inference: Evidence From Behavioral Predictions and Lay Theories of Behavior', *Personality and Social Psychology Bulletin*, vol. 28, no. 1, 2002, pp. 109–20, DOI: 10.1177/0146167202281010

48. Lao-Zi, *The Book of Lao Zi*, Foreign Language Press, 1993, p. 16.

49. Lin Yutang, *My Country and My People*, William Heinemann, 1936, p. 110.

50. US Department of State, 'Report on Global Anti-Semitism', 2005, https://2009-2017.state.gov/j/drl/rls/40258.htm

51. 'Anti-Semitism', *ADL*, https://www.adl.org/anti-semitism

52. Quoted in Moshe Zuckermann (ed.), *Tel Aviver Jahrbuch für deutsche Geschichte XXXIII, Antisemitismus, Antizionismus, Israelkritik* [Tel Aviv Yearbook for German History XXXIII, Antisemitism, Antizionism, Criticism of Israel], Wallerstein Verlag, 2005, p. 116.

53. 'Working Definition of Antisemitism' (PDF), *European Union Agency for Fundamental Rights*. Archived from the original (PDF) on 4 March 2011.

54. Quoted in Deborah E. Lipstadt, *Antisemitism Here and Now*, Schocken Books, 2019, p. 15.

55. Lipstadt, p. 15.

56. Lipstadt, p. 19.

57. Kenneth L. Marcus, 'The Definition of Antisemitism', in Charles Asher Small (ed.), *Global Antisemitism*, Charles Asher Small, ISGAP, Vol. 1, p. 111.

58. Ben Halpern, 'What Is Antisemitism?', *Modern Judaism—A Journal of Jewish Ideas and Experience*, vol. 1, iss. 3, December 1981, pp. 251–62, p. 260, https://doi.org/10.1093/mj/1.3.251

59. Shuchen Xiang, 'The Ghostly Other: Understanding Racism From Confucian and Enlightenment Models of Subjectivity', *Asian Philosophy*, vol. 25, no. 4, 2015, p. 392, https://doi.org/10.1080/09552367.2015.1105117

60. Aleks Philips, 'Jews in Hong Kong Watch Cautiously as the City Faces the Most Dramatic Protests This Century', *The Jewish Chronicle*, 11 November 2019, https://www.thejc.com/news/world/jews-in-hong-kong-watch-cautiously-as-the-city-faces-the-most-dramatic-protests-this-century-1.492932 (access date 1 February 2020).

8. THE STUDY OF ANTISEMITISM AND THE WESTERN MIND

1. Deborah E. Lipstadt, *Antisemitism Here and Now*, Schocken Books, 2019, p. 12.
2. Quoted in Lipstadt, pp. 12–13.
3. Lipstadt, pp. 12–13.
4. Isaac Chotiner, 'Looking at Anti-Semitism on the Left and the Right: An Interview With Deborah E. Lipstadt', *The New Yorker*, 24 January 2019, https://www.newyorker.com/news/the-new-yorker-interview/looking-at-anti-semitism-on-the-left-and-the-right-an-interview-with-deborah-e-lipstadt
5. Johann Hari, *Lost Connections: Uncovering the Real Causes of Depression*, Bloomsbury Circus, 2018, p. 220.
6. Richard E. Nisbett, *The Geography of Thought: How Asians and Westerners Think Differently … and Why*, Nicholas Brealey Publishing, 2015, p. xiiv.
7. Ibid., p. 109.
8. Ibid., p. 109.
9. Will Storr, 'How, Exactly, Do Our Brains Construct Reality?', *LitHub*, 11 March 2020, https://lithub.com/how-exactly-do-our-brains-construct-reality/ (access date 4 June 2002).
10. *Trupoyedstvo* ('eating of corpses') and *lyudoyedstvo* ('people eating').
11. Christopher L. Schilling, *Zen Judaism: The Case Against a Contemporary American Phenomenon*, Palgrave Macmillan, 2021, p. 87.
12. Elizabeth F. Howell, *Understanding and Treating Dissociative Identity Disorder: A Relational Approach*, Routledge, 2011, p. 57.
13. Dan Ariely and George Loewenstein, 'The Heat of the Moment: The Effect of Sexual Arousal on Sexual Decision Making', *Journal of Behavioral Decision Making*, vol. 19, no. 2, April 2006, pp. 87–98, https://doi.org/10.1002/bdm.501
14. Joseph Henrich, *The WEIRDest People in the World: How the West Became Psychologically Peculiar and Particularly Prosperous*, Farrar, Straus and Giroux, 2020, p. 52.

CONCLUSION

1. ADL/Global 100, https://global100.adl.org/country/singapore/2014
2. For an examination of the maintenance of religious harmony through law in Singapore, see, for instance: George Baylon Radics and Vineeta Sinha, 'Regulation of Religion and Granting of Public Holidays: The Case of Tai Pucam in Singapore,' *Asian Journal of Social Science*, vol. 46, no. 4/5, 2018, pp. 524–48, https://www.jstor.org/stable/26567263; George Baylon Radics and Poon Yee Suan, 'Amos Yee, Free Speech, and Maintaining Religious Harmony in Singapore,' *University of Pennsylvania Asian Law Review*, vol. 12, no. 2, 2016, pp. 140–185, https://scholarship.law.upenn.edu/cgi/viewcontent.cgi?article=1018&context=alr

SELECTED BIBLIOGRAPHY

Arudou, Debito, *Embedded Racism: Japan's Visible Minorities and Racial Discrimination*, Lanham, MD: Lexington Books, 2015.

Bartlett, Frederic C., *Remembering: A Study in Experimental and Social Psychology*, Cambridge, UK: Cambridge University Press, 1995 (first published 1932).

Behnke Kinney, Anne (ed.), *Chinese Views of Childhood*, Honolulu, HI: University of Hawai'i Press, 1995.

Beller, Steven, *Antisemitism: A Very Short Introduction*, Oxford: Oxford University Press, 2007.

Breen, John, and Mark Teeuwen, *A New History of Shinto*, Chichester, UK: Wiley-Blackwell, 2010.

Buruma, Ian, and Avishai Margalit, *Occidentalism: The West in the Eyes of Its Enemies*, New York: Penguin Press, 2004.

Clark, Herbert H., and Eve V. Clark, *Psychology and Language: An Introduction to Psycholinguistics*, New York: Harcourt Brace Jovanovich, 1977.

Cline, Erin M., *Families of Virtue: Confucian and Western Views on Childhood Development*, New York: Columbia University Press, 2015.

Cohen, R., *Negotiating Across Cultures: International Communication in an Interdependent World*, Washington, DC: United States Institute of Peace Press, 1997.

Davis, Bret W. (ed.), *The Oxford Handbook of Japanese Philosophy*, Oxford: Oxford University Press, 2020.

Dikötter, Frank, *The Discourse of Race in Modern China*, London: Hurst, 2015.

Donahue, Ray T., *Japanese Culture and Communication: Critical Cultural Analysis*, Lanham, MD; Oxford: University Press of America, 1998.

SELECTED BIBLIOGRAPHY

Dower, John W., *War Without Mercy: Race and Power in the Pacific War*, New York: Pantheon Books, 1987.

Duus, Masayo Umezawa, *Unlikely Liberators: The Men of the 100th and 442nd*, Honolulu, HI: University of Hawai'i Press, 2006.

Eber, Irene, *Jews in China, Cultural Conversations, Changing Perceptions*, University Park, PA: Pennsylvania State University Press, 2019.

Edelstein, Alan, *An Unacknowledged Harmony: Philo-Semitism and the Survival of European Jewry*, Westport, CT: Greenwood Press, 1982.

Ehrlich, Avrum (ed.), *Negotiating Identity Amongst the Religious Minorities of Asia*, Leiden/Boston, MA: E. J. Brill, 2009.

————— *Jews and Judaism in Modern China*, Abingdon, UK: Routledge, 2010.

Frost, Joe L., *A History of Children's Play and Play Environments*, New York, London: Routledge, 2009.

Gao, Bei, *Shanghai Sanctuary: Chinese and Japanese Policy Toward European Jewish Refugees During World War II*, Oxford: Oxford University Press, 2016.

Gelfand, M., *Rule Makers, Rule Breakers: Tight and Loose Cultures and the Secret Signals That Direct Our Lives*, New York: Scribner, 2019.

Gilman, Sander L., *Smart Jews: The Construction of the Image of Jewish Superior Intelligence*, Lincoln, NE: University of Nebraska Press, 1996.

Goldhagen, Daniel, *Hitler's Willing Executioners: Ordinary Germans and the Holocaust*, New York: Alfred A. Knopf, 1997.

Goldstein, Jonathan, *Jewish Identities in East and Southeast Asia: Singapore, Manila, Taipei, Harbin, Shanghai, Rangoon, and Surabaya* (New Perspectives on Modern Jewish History), Berlin: De Gruyter Oldenbourg, 2015.

Goodman, David G., and Masanori Miyazawa, *Jews in the Japanese Mind: The History and Uses of a Cultural Stereotype*, Lanham, MD: Lexington Books, 2000.

Goodman, Roger, *Japan's "International Youth"*, New York: Clarendon Press, 1990.

Hall, Edward T., *Beyond Culture*, New York: Anchor Books, 1976.

Henrich, Joseph, *The WEIRDest People in the World: How the West Became Psychologically Peculiar and Particularly Prosperous*, London: Farrar, Straus and Giroux, 2020.

Horvilleur, Delphine, *Anti-Semitism Revisited*, London: MacLehose Press, 2021.

Jaspers, Karl, *Origin and Goal of History*, London: Routledge Revivals, reprint 2011.

Jen, Gish, *Tiger Writing: Art, Culture, and the Interdependent Self*, Cambridge, MA: Harvard University Press, 2013.

SELECTED BIBLIOGRAPHY

Kawai, Hayao, *Dreams, Myths and Fairy Tales in Japan*, Einsiedeln, Switzerland: Daimon, 1995.

Lassner, Phyllis, and Lara Trubowitz (eds), *Antisemitism and Philosemitism in the Twentieth and Twenty-First Centuries: Representing Jews, Jewishness, and Modern Culture*, Newark, DE: University of Delaware Press, 2008.

Levenson, Alan, *Between Philosemitism and Antisemitism: Defenses of Jews and Judaism in Germany, 1871-1932*, Lincoln, NE: University of Nebraska Press, 2004.

Lipstadt, Deborah E., *Antisemitism Here and Now*, New York: Schocken Books, 2019.

Makino, Seiichi, and Michio Tsutsui, *A Dictionary of Basic Japanese Grammar*, Tokyo: The Japan Times Publishing, 2020.

Marcus, Kenneth L., *The Definition of Anti-Semitism*, Oxford: Oxford University Press, 2015.

Medzini, Meron, *Under the Shadow of the Rising Sun: Japan and the Jews During the Holocaust Era*, Boston, MA: Academic Studies Press, 2016.

Moffic, H. Steven, et al., *Anti-Semitism and Psychiatry*, Cham, Switzerland: Springer, 2020.

Mushkat, Marian, *Philosemitic and Anti-Jewish Attitudes in Post-Holocaust Poland*, Lewiston, NY: Edwin Mellen Press, 1992.

Myers, Brian R., *The Cleanest Race: How North Koreans See Themselves – And Why It Matters*, New York: Melville House, 2010.

Nisbett, Richard E., *The Geography of Thought: How Asians and Westerners Think Differently … and Why*, Boston, MA: Nicholas Brealey Publishing, 2005.

Okri, Ben, *Birds of Heaven*, London: Phoenix, 1996.

Owyang, Sharon, *Frommer's Shanghai*, Hoboken, NJ: Wiley Publishing, 2007.

Ross, James, and Song Lihong (eds), *The Image of Jews in Contemporary China* (Jewish Identities in Post-Modern Society), Boston, MA: Academic Studies Press, 2016.

Rubinstein, William, and Hilary Rubinstein, *Philosemitism: Admiration and Support in the English-Speaking World for Jews, 1840–1939*, Basingstoke, UK: Macmillan, 1999.

Rummel, R. J., *China's Bloody Century: Genocide and Mass Murder Since 1900*, London: Routledge, 2017.

Schilling, Christopher L., *Zen Judaism: The Case Against a Contemporary American Phenomenon*, Cham, Switzerland: Palgrave Macmillan, 2021.

Shih, H., *Chung-kuo che-hsueh shi ta-kang* (An Outline of the History of Chinese Philosophy), Shanghai: Commercial Press, 1919.

SELECTED BIBLIOGRAPHY

Shillony, Ben-Ami, *The Jews and the Japanese: The Successful Outsiders*, North Clarendon, VT: Charles E. Tuttle Company, 1992.

Shin, Gi-Wook. *Ethnic Nationalism in Korea: Genealogy, Politics, and Legacy*, Stanford, CA: Stanford University Press, 2006.

Simmel, Ernst, *Anti-Semitism: A Social Disease*, New York: International Universities Press, 1946.

Slezkine, Yuri, *The Jewish Century*, Princeton, NJ: Princeton University Press, 2019.

Sterckx, Roel, *Ways of Heaven: An Introduction to Chinese Thought*, New York: Basic Books, 2019.

Storr, Will, *The Science of Storytelling*, London: William Collins, 2019.

Stretcher, Victor J., *Life on Purpose*, New York: Harper One, 2016.

Watts, Alan, *Tao: The Watercourse Way*, New York: Pantheon, 1977.

Weiss, Bari, *How to Fight Anti-Semitism*, London: Penguin, 2020.

Wimpfheimer, Barry Scott, *The Talmud: A Biography* (Lives of Great Religious Books), Princeton, NJ: Princeton University Press, 2018.

Žižek, Slavoj, *In Defense of Lost Causes*, London: Verso, 2008.

INDEX

INDEX

INDEX

INDEX